Welcome to the EVERYTHING. Series!

These handy, accessible books give you all you need to tackle a difficult project, gain a new hobby, comprehend a fascinating topic, prepare for an exam, or even brush up on something you learned back in school but have since forgotten.

You can choose to read an Everything® book from cover to cover or just pick out the information you want from our four useful boxes: e-questions, e-facts, e-alerts, and e-ssentials. We give you everything you need to know on the subject, but throw in a lot of fun stuff along the way too.

We now have more than 400 Everything® books in print, spanning such wide-ranging categories as weddings, pregnancy, cooking, music instruction, foreign language, crafts, pets, New Age, and so much more. When you're done reading them all, you can finally say you know Everything®!

PUBLISHER Karen Cooper

MANAGING EDITOR Lisa Laing

COPY CHIEF Casey Ebert

PRODUCTION EDITOR Jo-Anne Duhamel

ACQUISITIONS EDITOR Lisa Laing

DEVELOPMENT EDITOR Lisa Laing

COVER DESIGNER Frank Rivera

Visit the entire Everything® series at www.everything.com

THE EVERYTHING®

Mindful Word Search Book

VOLUME 1

75 Uplifting Puzzles to
Reduce Stress, Improve Focus,
and Sharpen Your Mind

Positive Affirmations and Inspiring Messages
TO HELP YOU RELAX AND REFLECT

Charles Timmerman
Founder of Funster.com

Adams Media
New York London Toronto Sydney New Delhi

Dedication

Dedicated to my family who have provided so many moments of happiness.

Adams Media
An Imprint of Simon & Schuster, Inc.
57 Littlefield Street
Avon, Massachusetts 02322

An Everything® Series Book.
Everything® and everything.com® are registered trademarks of Simon & Schuster, Inc.

First Adams Media trade paperback edition November 2020

ADAMS MEDIA and colophon are trademarks of Simon & Schuster.

For information about special discounts for bulk purchases, please contact Simon & Schuster Special Sales at 1-866-506-1949 or business@simonandschuster.com.

The Simon & Schuster Speakers Bureau can bring authors to your live event. For more information or to book an event contact the Simon & Schuster Speakers Bureau at 1-866-248-3049 or visit our website at www.simonspeakers.com.

Interior design by Michelle Kelly

Manufactured in the United States of America

10 9 8 7 6 5 4 3 2 1

ISBN 978-1-5072-1467-1

Contains material adapted from the following titles published by Adams Media, an Imprint of Simon & Schuster, Inc.: *365 Ways to Live Happy* by Meera Lester, copyright © 2010, ISBN 978-1-60550-028-7; *365 Ways to Reduce Stress* by Eve Adamson, copyright © 2009, ISBN 978-1-4405-0025-1; *The Everything® Guide to Chakra Healing* by Heidi E. Spear, copyright © 2011, ISBN 978-1-4405-2584-1; *The Everything® Guide to Meditation for Healthy Living* by David B. Dillard-Wright, PhD, and Ravinder Jerath, MD, copyright © 2011, ISBN 978-1-4405-1088-5; *The Everything® Zen Book* by Jacky Sach and Jessica Faust, copyright © 2004, ISBN 978-1-58062-973-7; *My Pocket Meditations* by Meera Lester, copyright © 2017, ISBN 978-1-5072-0341-5; *My Pocket Positivity* by Courtney E. Ackerman, copyright © 2018, ISBN 978-1-5072-0850-2; *Rituals for Life* by Meera Lester, copyright © 2017, ISBN 978-1-5072-0524-2.

Acknowledgments

I would like to thank Lisa Laing at Simon & Schuster, whose many talents made this book possible.

Contents

Introduction

Concentrating on a word search grid and methodically searching for words can be as effective as meditation for relieving stress. *The Everything® Mindful Word Search Book, Volume 1* takes this activity one step further. Each puzzle is constructed with words that are contained in a quote that explores some aspect of mindfulness. With guided meditations, positive affirmations, and reflections on gratitude, self-realization, and happiness, you'll find a treasure trove of mindful activities as well as entertaining and diverting puzzles.

The puzzles in this book are in the traditional word search format. The words you will be searching for are underlined in the quotes, affirmations, and meditations. Words are hidden in the puzzles in any direction: up, down, forward, backward, or diagonal. The words are always found in a straight line, and letters are never skipped. Words may overlap. For example, the two letters at the end of the word

MAST could be used as the start of the word *STERN*. Only uppercase letters are used, and any spaces in an entry are removed. For example, *LAW OF ATTRACTION* would be found in the puzzle as *LAWOFATTRACTION*. Apostrophes and hyphens are also omitted in the puzzles. Draw a circle around each word you find. Then highlight the word in the quote so you will know which words remain to be found.

A favorite word search strategy is to look for the first letter in a word, then see if the second letter is one of the neighboring letters, and so on until the word is found. Or instead of searching for the first letter in a word, it is sometimes easier to look for letters that stand out, like *Q*, *U*, *X*, and *Z*. Double letters in a word will also stand out and be easier to find. Another strategy is to simply scan each row, column, and diagonal looking for any words.

When you finish mindfully solving the puzzles, don't toss the book! Keep it as a resource so you can open it at any time to find seventy-five ways to be mindful, express gratitude, and increase your happiness.

PUZZLES

CHOOSE TO THINK HAPPY THOUGHTS

If you want to find **happiness** and add **years** to your **life**, think happy thoughts. When you choose **positive** thoughts over negative ones, **you** are more **likely** to develop an optimistic **outlook** on life. According to happiness **researchers** such as Martin E.P. Seligman, director of the Positive Psychology **Center** at the University of Pennsylvania, and Barbara Fredrickson, PhD, **professor** of **psychology** at the University of North Carolina at Chapel **Hill**, positive **people** generally have **higher** levels of optimism and life satisfaction and live **longer**. In a BBC News report, Dr. Seligman was **quoted** as saying that he believed that "we have compelling **evidence** that **optimists** and **pessimists** will differ markedly in how long they live." Dr. Fredrickson has **counseled** that changing your **mindset** can change your **body** chemistry. She has stated that positive **feelings** literally can **open** the **heart** and mind. And there's more **good** news. **Even** if you aren't **normally** a happy **person**, thinking happy **thoughts** is a **skill** that can be learned. Work on **being** open, being an optimist, **choosing** to think positive thoughts, and seeing the **proverbial** glass half **full** rather than half empty. The **next** time you are in **line** at the post office and **someone** cuts in front of you or says something rude, resist the urge to **respond** with anger, which can **clamp** down your **blood** vessels and **increase** your blood pressure. **Instead**, return rudeness with **kindness** and respect. Keep that positive **vibe** going through your intentions and **actions** in whatever you do. The more frequently you **choose** to be happy, the more your **effort** will be strengthened. So don't **fret**; be happy and live longer.

```
K W C E P S S E N I P P A H V D P C F T
H P B B I K R Y K C L A M P O E Y U U C
T I P R O V E R B I A L E O S O L H M F
V Y G O L O H C Y S P S G N I L E E F F
R Z L H X I C H O O S I N G Z A B I T Q
C R P Y E A R S T I N T T E R F Y N Q C
R Q D U D R A E M E O H S T X Z O S Y R
M S K L E Q E I O L I F E I L R D T Q F
L I K E L Y S G R L T N N Y M N U E O I
A U X N E T E V L N C Z I A O I I A U T
Q N R R S M R B B S A E L P P U T D T O
L P P K N I E N L L S L S E P E O P L E
S A I S U N O U O O Y E R V I B R O O N
Q L B B O D P N O J R S N I O O R S O Z
L K N E C S G H D T O C D D F D S I K Q
C P M I F E C F K N F T E E N Y M T J E
K O P N R T H O U G H T S N T I E I G I
S P P G X I N C R E A S E C T O K V T Y
C S S E Z M P E F F O R T E U E U E E K
N Y N K N D T Q I R O V W X B A R Q U N
```

Solution on page 164

AWAKENING:
THE ALTERNATING BREATH

This **breathing** exercise is **taught** in nearly all **yoga** schools and **styles** as an "**awakening**" technique to **vitalize** both **body** and **mind**. Often used as a **prelude** to **meditation**, its **Sanskrit** name is Anuloma **Viloma**. With it, **you** also place your **active** hand in a **gesture** known as the **Vishnu Mudra** ("sign of **preservation**"). The **index** and middle fingers are **tucked** into the **palm** of the **hand**, leaving the thumb, third **finger**, and little finger open. You will be using the **thumb** to close the right **nostril**, and the third and **little** fingers to close the **left** nostril. The steps of the exercise are as **follows**:

1. **Start** with an **upright** spine. Place your active hand in the Vishnu Mudra.

2. **Close** the right nostril with the thumb, **inhale** deeply through the left nostril.

3. Close **both** nostrils, hold in your breath to the count of **eight**.

4. **Release** the right nostril; **exhale** slowly.

5. Keeping the left nostril closed, inhale **deeply** through the right nostril.

6. Close both nostrils; hold in your breath to the **count** of eight.

7. Release the left nostril; exhale **slowly**.

```
Z U E V N M D M X G T O Q W I B M E S W
H H D W E Y P A J B O H F P U T Y H R A
B J U F W U Y E J C X Y G T H G X W C E
G C L F H N X T H G I R P U G B W Z O L
A U E H D V O J I F F W M B A Z Q E U Z
L G R Z V G F N E R E B L E F T I I N S
O L P X I M K A W A K E N I N G S O T N
O U J G Y L M R N U R S K D H Q B Y W S
I G N I H T A E R B L D N T L C L O S E
D N P Y J P E T D I T I U A G E T X D G
M B D Y L R U K I I K N U M S K E U O Y
F M E G E P H J O V T H I D U B L X C A
S B X G P R E S E R V A T I O N A K A M
H A N D A E U E M L M L T T S X H C C O
Z I G P L L T T D T I E H I W E X S T L
F N K O M E U M S T N R G T O D E T I I
N X Y N Y A C Y T E D U T O L N G A V V
X Y S D B S K L A Z G H J S L I C R E X
F B Q H D E E K D A Y Y Y L W O L S T Z G
P H F R R I D G O Z U K S C F N D L A V
```

Solution on page 164

THREE TIMES A DAY, VISUALIZE ACHIEVING A PERSONAL GOAL

What's your **primary** personal **goal**? Is it to **lose** weight, **spend** less, or **earn** more **money**? **Whatever** it is, **write** out an **affirmation** for **achieving** it. For **example**: "From **now** on at **mealtimes** I will **eat** one-third less than my **usual** serving of **food**, and I will **walk** for thirty **minutes** each **weekday**." Try to **keep** your affirmation **succinct** and to the **point**, so it **will** be **easy** to recall. Repeat it at least **three** times **during** the day. The more **specific** your affirmation, the **more** effective it will be in **helping** you **attain** your goal.

```
X M C I O E A O A I O J H C L C K I M Y
N Q Q L F C G E M C R Z G N A L J F Z W
R P H R J M D J L T X F G G A V L L T R
J Y X U V W N R P P X F V W V F R P V S
A F B A Q F H K J B M C H Q H I N Y F K
M G B Z F K A P P Y S A E B N O A F G E
Z F A R N F H G E X T H X I X O U N A V
K J Q X V G I H P E B G A E Z Q O C Z U
G Q B W N K E R V Y K T S K J W C O G T
S E M I T L A E M N T M H U J I Y O Z C
D N R M P E R O M A R G I W J L A R T F
K U E I D B N C V F T N R N I L D R F L
D J N F U O N N T C N I C C U S K P O R
F G Y Q O U A F X P T V O W Z T E S Q D
R D V L G O Y D O E R E E N Q P E U L E
F J M J T N D I C I F I C E P S W S C Y
U R A M Q A N A B H F H M N R J D U Z S
C Y R E K T E B M L J C R A P H H A O J
F Y N B C A P B A X G A T D R F T L I V
C Q I J J J X S X W G E M P C P Y E N O M
```

Solution on page 164

SMILE MORE OFTEN

Force **yourself** to **smile**. **Try** it; it's not that **difficult**. Now **hold** it for a **count** of **ten** and **deepen** it. **Mentally** affirm, "I am **happy**, totally, **blissfully** happy." **Notice** how your **mood** begins to **shift**. You can't **help** but **feel** a **little** lighter. **Use** your smile to **start** a happiness **epidemic**. Smile at **everyone**, everywhere. **People** are **hardwired** to **respond** to the **facial** expressions they encounter. If you **glower** at someone, that **person** will return a **frown**, but your smile will **evoke** a smile. You'll feel happier too, because your **body** responds to your smile, **even** if you are **faking** the **grin**. So fake it until you **genuinely** feel happy. **Once** you know it **works**, do it often.

```
M N N J W B E P Y G G K C F Q V A I G D
I S Q O S O A P N N P L I U U U N I N P
X I W X P Q R A I Z H H S S S N K R M K
Y A M W X P U K D D N O P S E R O U S T
M Z T G P X A B S T E H L T Y V O Q M M
N E Q R G F T O C T K M M D L F O W I O
I D C F H L Z H A R D W I R E D B K L A
N A Z E F I K U E G A S M C N L P L E H
E J N P Q T M T L U C I F F I D M N J Z
W V K R I T M O G E Z L A S U E E C N O
D G T X V L W T M R E C S P N V K X Z G
A H M N T E N W N S I F B T E Q B C A N
E Q A H R H G B R A U N A R G O B N O J
I K Z P Y K J U L L G L Y G D F P S W D
O D B B P W O J L H L O Q Y K B R L O E
D U E Q G Y D Y B Y N O T I C E M O E V
M C C O Y D E E P E N F E S P O M S W E
M M S U G Y R J I C I I E B H F U S N N
E P S A Q B K S N H T V S Q E I L N M T
D R T L D Z E Q S K K T Q Q G T R A T S
```

Solution on page 165

FEEL LIFE FORCE

Are you **familiar** with **feeling** your life-force **energy**? If not, **try** this **simple** exercise. **Hold** your **arms** out to the **sides** and rapidly **wiggle** your **fingers** and **shake** your hands in the **air**. Shake and **wave** your **hands**. Count to **thirty** as you do this. Then **suddenly** stop. **Notice** what you feel. Do **you** feel a **tingling**? Do you feel **vibration**? That's life-force energy. **Spend** more time **evaluating** your energy **level**. Spend **time** noticing how **others** make you feel. Who in your life **fills** you up? Who **makes** you feel **tired**? It's not **always** just what they say or how they say it; people's energy **fields** interact with yours. Your **electromagnetic** field can be **scientifically** measured. It's **real**.

```
T F H T A Y Q Y V Z X C T O N R Y T J R
M G X C U C Y L N E D D U S Y N E Z E S
K A Y O E M O Q C E M K C L J M U O Y G
S P R A I L I M A F R I F X E W X A P S
F G F I N G E R S C E J X V E V W F A Q
S C K D P Z U C O N A U Y I V L E Y D H
K G Q Q F D R E T N L O R J A E R L W Z
N H E M E D O I H R T I N G L I N G A J
S X W R D K F A E Y O R I I U L N R V D
N E I W A I N C R W N M N R A Y M S E U
P T G J C D C N S A C G A F T S P E M M
N X G A S P R L B Z Z F M G I E I H A W
Y R L U M N L C X Q Y G R E N E F D K I
K L E I Q I K B Y T J O E D G E F B E E
Y U U V F D T N R P L T C F X N T E S S
T Q K R U T L I Y K N O I T A R B I V I
P H M X F E H Z M R R E T B Y Q M G C D
K A U P Q T L S A E L M O Q G P B R L G
D Y A H K V C L F D G I N B L U I O Y J
O E T D E A V D S T X R C E K A H S H N
```

Solution on page 165

PRAISE YOURSELF

You **praise** your **children**, your **friends**, your **coworkers**, and your **spouse** whenever **they** **accomplish** something praiseworthy, so why not **give** yourself a one-minute praising for your own **achievements**? You're not **being** a braggart or **egotistical** when you **acknowledge** some **wonderful** task you completed or breakthrough you made **during** your day. You **undoubtedly** work **very** hard and **probably** accomplish **much** that no one but you **recognizes**. If you **finally** played a complicated **piano** sonata all the way **through** or found an **ingenious** way to **increase** the **family** budget, tell **yourself** how wonderfully **brilliant** and accomplished you are. **Bask** in the **glory** of that **moment**. You **deserve** it.

T P R B H R G C S P O U S E C M H C W Q
R J F T N O N A I P S D F V N P S W Z W
W R E E Y L I M A F N D O I P E T U F S
Z I Q P O P R A I E X P Q G Z E N L T D
R G Y R K S U O I N E G N I J D E O E I
F R X A A I D R H B G P N I O S M S R K
X J F I K I F U F L P G N U R O E F B L
P K B S R E K R O W O C B U M R V H A L
C T H E Y G P R Y C R T O E V A E C S R
X Q S E I B Y N E E E Y N E F G I U K J
O N B A Y N F R A D A T V L D T H M D G
I V C A L M G S L I V D U E S B C E M P
Q U U F B E E Y C B N F L I R H A G H J
A Y G I A F F Z U D R W T I I Y H M R B
H S H N B G H M N E O O L L W Y H X Z X
E W K A O J W Q D N G L D B X S C I T M
F Y U L R D W N K E I R C Z B D W Z H M
H S I L P M O C C A E J V Q Q Y J J F L
S Z T Y N W A T N N O N E C H Q D R E S
B E R O J S T T H R O U G H E X P I J L

Solution on page 165

HEALING ON ALL LEVELS

According to chakra theory, when all the chakras are balanced, your body, mind, intuition, and the part of you that is eternal (soul, spirit, source energy, etc.) all work together. At these times, each chakra is functioning well: You sense the state of your body, you express your creative ideas, you have energy to follow through on commitments, your heart is open to receive with appropriate boundaries, you are authentic in your communication, you look clearly and objectively at your thought patterns and habits, and you listen to the quiet place inside.

When this happens, what you believe, think, say, and do line up, and you can manifest what you want in your life. You are in sync with your body, your mind, and source energy, which connects you to all life and the energy of the Universe. It is through this, your connection to universal energy, that you are able to manifest your desires and work on deeply healing physical, mental, and emotional wounds.

```
F R E U F T V I D E I Z N I D O T P I L
S P S U X L M D S X W Y Z U O K U R I N
M N D N T G F E M E S N E S C N Y S H O
D U E E W J H A R K A H C H S F T C L N
K H I P S T N E M T I M M O C E A W N U
W U Y F P I Y O D Q P W Z A N E R F W N
Q O B T F A R Z I L W Y Y T V N U P A I
L B R A U T H E N T I C L I J N E E X V
A F U K C M K K S T A G E R C V F C A E
T Z O T N C T J R P C C V T A X O B T R
N O Y C Y O O R P Y E E I W K E L T N S
E Z P R I D I R A R G O T N V E L J B E
M L M E T N O T D E N R C Q U Q O C A V
P A I A O P D B I I H E E E T M W L L E
V N N T R T W G N U N A J N N Q M L A I
L R D I L O I G C I T G B V E E R O N L
I E A V F N P R L L A N O I T O M E C E
F T D E H E A L I N G M I A T R A P E B
E E K Y K C S B T P V D T G V S X A D K
Q T H G U O H T X W S S U K B P G K A K
```

Solution on page 166

CONSIDER WHAT YOUR BODY CAN DO

Have you ever **thought** about **everything** your **body** can do? If you have, you **know** what it **means** when **people** say that our bodies are **absolutely**, astoundingly **capable**. If you **find** yourself **spending** a lot of time **thinking** about what your body can't do or what your body **looks** like, give this **exercise** a try. You can **practice** it **anytime**, but you might find it most **helpful** after a **workout** or other **physical** activity.

If you **just** completed a workout, went for a run, or even just **chased** your kids around the **yard**, take a few **minutes** to think about all the work that activity **entailed**. Note each **individual** action that **needed** to happen for you to **accomplish** what you did.

For **example**, if you **played** tag with your **children**, consider that you needed to be able to **stand**, walk, run, **shift** direction, **move** while looking behind you, **modulate** your **speed** as needed to **escape** (or to allow a **young** child to **catch** you), and most **likely** the ability to talk and **laugh** while **doing** all of these things.

As **adults**, we get so **used** to what our bodies can do that we stop feeling **grateful** for all of it. Now that you have a **list** of all the things your body just did during a particular **activity**, practice **being** grateful for each and every **ability**. Thank your body for **empowering** you to do something **meaningful**, like play with your children.

```
G O L I K E L Y H M P N L L Z O L C M U
S D E K S U N F A N Y T I M E V A F L S
C M O M F T H J C X K S H E L P M A X E
W O I P N Z U P C F T D H O A W A G A D
P V L D V S T U O K R O W B U X T O D D
H E S E T U N I M V M V L R E G N U O Y
H C C L T N E M P O W E R I N G H S L Q
T P T I A B S O L U T E L Y T M J T U E
I H N A T U G N I H T Y R E V E L A F H
D G I T C C D A S K O O L Y H A R N E P
Q U J N L Y A I H F N O Q T H N Q D T A
W A N E K A O R V X E Y T I V I T C A R
B L E G S I C C P I R A I L F N F Q R L
M F E N W I N I B O D Y R I V G E G G O
V P D P D Q C G S U L N N B T F I H S D
Q G E R A H F R L Y I D I A H U Q O B W
P N D O A C X T E Z H M O D U L A T E X
W I H S P Y S W T X C P L A Y E D N I N
O O E D Q L B E S P E N D I N G W O N K
I D W K K M E A N S P E E D D X W C G F
```

Solution on page 166

QUIET YOUR MIND BEFORE STARTING YOUR DAY

Focus on your **thinking** at the **start** of every **day**. Are your **thoughts** already **racing** through your to-do **list**? Are they **jumping** from one **subject** to **another** through thought **associations**? Did a troubling **dream** leave you **anxious** or angry or fearful upon **awakening**? If you **answered** yes to any of those **questions**, spend ten **minutes** before you even get out of bed doing a **mental** check-in. Take deep **breaths** and be **aware** of your entire **body**. Feel **anchored** and **centered** in it. **Quiet** your mind. Think **positive** thoughts. Dial out the **emotions** of bad dreams and the anxieties associated with the day **ahead**. **Relax** into peace. The **world** can **wait** for ten minutes.

```
L U V F A S L I K Z N Q S T M Y N V S F
G R P W E W O X Q U G U Y Z T B X R F Z
I X A Y M S A S U M D E R O H C N A K L
L R Y Z G L S K I A N S W E R E D G U Z
E F Y J E T S G E S G T U V L H I M O L
S M B R T U O N T N N I M I N U T E S A
N L H R B Z C I U C I O S T H G U O H T
P T A J E R I K E G P N C I D Y U Q K N
W T E Q R A A N L I M S G S D T R T W E
S C A X X D T I U C U F F O C U S I A M
T D W L Y E I H V O J R B P P I K A K P
J T W I R M O T S X A H U T L V H W W H
T C H E D O N P X C D X J Q V T Y T P B
R J D R A T S A I R V J B Y S Z C K R G
D V E E Y I N N V D D J G D B J P G O O
K A H O W O G X T L L T Y V I H Z Y F C
M L E E T N N I R U V I I H L Q W E L O
W G D H S S Q O R G C G Y X O S F G C L
E M E S A O W U A C K M N U Q L I U X G
L R T K Y G L S S W E T N P O R K W A C
```

Solution on page 166

CONDUCT A MORNING CHAKRA CHECK-IN AND INTENTION-SETTING RITUAL

Adding a **chakra** check-in and **intention**-setting **period** to your **morning** is a great way to be **mindful** of how you **want** to feel **during** your day. **After** you have **washed** your face and **brushed** your teeth, take a **moment** to see how you are **feeling**, and set an intention. The intention you set can **come** from what you **notice** in the moment about your chakras. For **example**, if you feel that your **heart** is heavy this morning, set an intention such as "**Today** my heart is well, **open**, and **strong**," and **visualize** sending healing **energy** to your heart **space**. Use that as your **mantra** for the day. **Write** your intention on a piece of **paper** and bring it with you. You can put it in your **pocket**, tape it to the back of your **phone**, or tape it to the **dashboard** of your car. If you put it **somewhere** where you'll see it, then you'll have an **easier** time **remembering** it **throughout** your day.

If you are feeling **ungrounded** and separate from your body, sit on the **floor** and **notice** that you are held up by the **earth**. Or stand tall and feel your feet firmly **connected** to the earth. Then say to yourself, "All day I am safe, **stable**, and connected." Feel the **support** of the earth underneath you.

Repeat the intention **three** times, with your eyes **closed**, envisioning it to be true. As you **envision** it as true, you are creating that **reality**. If you think you'll be anxious all day, then it would be hard for you to feel **otherwise**. When you notice an **imbalance** in your psychology or **physical** body in the morning, ask **yourself** which chakra that connects to, then set your intention in a way that supports that chakra's **function**.

```
R R S N D E J E Y T I L A E R O W I B R
J B V B A E C K W D O B H Q L G P A T G
O O E R B A H I H S E J C M D P I R O N
L C T E P U A S T I D H O A L H M K T I
U H G S R D N A U O K R S D E I B A Q L
R V W O P H B G I R N H U A Q V A H X E
A M O T E L T R R I B R R P W F L C Z E
U L Z P E T E P N O I T C N U F A G O F
F C U R E P I G A N U D E T C E N N O C
F Y X F G N R G P G N Z J R I C M T G
X Z M V D D D A W A E S D E R T E I H G
Y L S I E N S U P P O R T E N O H P E T
T G M S J O I A V M E F B A D P Z X R D
S C O U P I O M E I A M W Z W H Y S W Q
D L M A E T W W S T E K C O P Y J M I T
C Q E L N N H A S M G N O R T S G A S P
R P N I E E E P E C L N O I S I V N E Y
J M T Z R T H R O U G H O U T C W T K J
V I C E G N Q M Y G E U T O D A Y R R Q
A F H T Y I E Z R Y O U R S E L F A A F
```

Solution on page 167

PHOTOGRAPHY AS MANIFESTATION

Taking **photographs** can be a **meditative** and manifestation **practice**. You **focus** on the **object** and on getting a **particular** representation of it. In this focused **inquiry**, you're **able** to become **present** to what is and your **relationship** to what you're photographing, disregarding what else **might** be going on in **life** or what your next "have-to" might be.

You can use photography as part of your **manifestation**. Be **intentional** about what you photograph or what photograph you **choose** to own. Then, put the photographs on a **collage**, on your **altar**, or in your **wallet** as **inspiration**. It can be a **literal** representation of what you **desire**, or a representation of an **action** you hope to **experience** one day. It can also be a photograph of **anything** that brings you **bliss**, inspiration, **hope**, comfort, joy, or any feeling **associated** with the **chakras** that you want to **strengthen**. Photography is a **powerful** tool. It demonstrates to your **eyes** that what you want is manifested in **physical** reality.

T C H Z T S L G D E S I R E A F P P Q M
M H H E E Y R S P R A T L A G K R H F E
W A P O L H E W K K D N R N E A E T X V
J K A F L T S T T V F O O E H A S E V I
Z R E L A T I O N S H I P C N Y E I E O
B A W Z W Y H I I U T T H C E G N G E A
L S G N I H T Y N A R A O C E X T K C J
I L O E G W L V T Q A R T J H K B H N S
S N D Z G H N S E U L I O L L O E Y E S
S T Q D J A E T N C U P G U V H O H I N
N K S U E F L L T R C S R F F F B S R F
N E M O I V A L I C I N A R Q L S N E B
Z Q J N B R I F O L T I P E P A P E P L
F Y A O E J Y T N C R L H W N C C T X D
D M C T H T E G A B A S S O C I A T E D
S W I I U F I C L T P M P P T S L Z L J
I L A Q I I T P T C I D X C P Y U O B P
X E G L E I P S C G X D A D Y H P C A O
C C F Z O L U O H X G R E N E P O H O P
S Y K N A Q K T G R P B J M D N C N R F

Solution on page 167

PRACTICING ONE-BREATH MEDITATION

Everyday life **continually** poses challenges to our **inner** peace. In the **midst** of a stressful **episode**, whether at **home** or at work, we **often** long for the **peaceful** moments that a **secluded**, quiet **meditation** offers. But the real **world** doesn't offer such **moments** when they're most **needed**. We have to **create** them. At these times, a **conscious** pause can **refresh** the body and **mind** just as well as an **extended** meditation **session**. All that's needed is the **desire** to stop and take **action**—or no action as the **case** may be. If you find **yourself** at a **standstill** at work, feeling that you've come to the end of the rope you're **climbing**, stop. Remind yourself that this is an **opportune** time for momentary meditation, to refresh and **relax** your mind from the climb. **Pause** all **thoughts** and remind yourself that your inner peace **prevails** at this moment. Think of that peace as a **place** within you. **Straighten** your spine as you do this, and lift your **chin** upward. **Focus** your eyes above your head, at the **ceiling** or wall. Take a conscious breath, **slowly** and deliberately. Think of your place of peace **opening** its door as the air fills your lungs. On **exhaling**, appreciate the moment for allowing you to pause, and **return** to the work at hand.

```
Z L Y L W O L S N C J U R H O J J C J V
G U U Y O E T L O U L O K J W G S S O Z
Z B R F A N C S D W P U C R Z U K D R I
R X M R E D E U B P E Q H Q C V X E Z N
X J I M G C Y J O X G M M O F W D S O N
Y C O H L S A R T A D N F I K N A I D E
Q M H U P N T E E U Y L I C G X T R L R
D X D I Q U N S P V E E S L X C Q E R V
E E R M N D A S S S E L Q I A N G E O O
D E Y E E C K A R T I T S M B H T T W G
E B H D F Y L U U A R B U B I U X A X O
E Z O I N R O Z V N Z A O I R M G E O Q
N N M T P Y E E Z D S X I N S I N R P A
X U E A K Q R S R S T F C G T D I C E V
A H U T Z P F R H T K G S H H S L P N Z
L S U I F S E S S I O N N J G T I H I U
E N Y O G O U C J L K D O S U S E D N V
R C O N T I N U A L L Y C K O X C N G H
O F L F K V V J R L H M F D H G Y I Q L
O O Y F R L K E X Y P E E B T B D M D V
```

Solution on page 167

RETREAT WITHIN TO CLEAR YOUR MIND

Plan a little **time** off just for **yourself** to do some inner **reflection**. The **amount** of time is not as **important** as getting the **respite** you need. Make your time away a **priority**. It's a **small** amount of time just for you to **clear** your head, **gather** your **energy**, and get **perspective**. Retreat to someplace **peaceful** where you can **relax** and have a **break** from the **responsibilities** of work and **family**. Don't **know** of any great **retreat** places? Take your **favorite** book and head to a **beach**. If there's no **ocean** in your **backyard**, find a **shady** bank along the **edge** of a lake, **creek**, river, or **pond**—someplace where the **earth** and **water** meet. **Sink** into your beach **chair**, tune into the **sounds** of **nature**, open your **book**, and lose yourself in the **story**. Or, just sit back, **close** your eyes, and let your mind **wander**. You don't have to do **anything** while on your retreat except make a **space** for **tranquility** and joy to **fill** you.

```
R S R P Y B Y Y N U C K L B R E A K N E
X A L E R B P B Y T R T A P E E D G E V
T V M N S L R L P R R A T Y E A N A O C
T U P N J P I Y W A N D E R A N C T L L
Y W Y Z N M O V P N F I L L U A P H V Z
M O D I A Z R N F Q L I M P C H P E T P
C K Y F J C I O S U L B A C K Y A R D V
B L X G E J T E V I T C E P S R E P Q T
W Q O Z R Z Y L N L B S T S K F D J N O
U T C S R E T U M I F I N P L Z B M S Q
S E O O E V N F D T R F L E S R U O Y A
C W T P T S D E Z Y D A C I Y Y R P O S
B L Q B R E M C T K N T T M T U D G N K
T W B H E E W A E I I N Q P P I N A E O
T U F C A S S E L O R U I O D I E R H S
S D A M T O R P N L M O V R H C U S A S
E P K O U C D T I M E M V T O T M X W I
S I R N Y N K W I T Z A Y A A C R X I N
R Y D N O N H O F Q E N M N F J C A L K
X S Q P K W B J C H A I R T C W A T E R
```

Solution on page 168

NOURISH YOUR INNER BEING

Nourish your **inner** being by **diving** into **meditative** reflection, **centering** and **grounding** yourself, and **endeavoring** to deepen the **experience**. **According** to **Harvard** scientist Herbert Benson, who has **conducted** studies on **Buddhist** meditation and the **effects** of the **mind** on the **body**, when you turn **inward** through meditation, **complex** activity in the **brain** (as seen on MRI brain **scans**) takes place. That **activity** actually **calms** the body, reduces **stress** levels, and promotes **healing**. Eventually a period of **quietude** is **reached** and as your **concentration** deepens, you experience a **disconnect** between the body and mind. Some **people** describe that experience as one of **awesome** peace and **joy**.

```
S W C A V P W H G N A A Z L X M C H P G
Q R L S D E T C U D N O C M A Z I C G G
V V R H A R V A R D R A W N I S P E A H
Y Q P Z I C P I P F Q L J I T N C I E H
H T I W S S E R T S G O D T O Y D A J G
C G T M L R S M L A C N X U G T L S N M
A T R E U H Y R C K T T I N X I Q T X S
I R D O W R N W C Y V I I R N V O C E F
W U E Q U I E T U D E R D G E I L E L G
B A H V E N D I S C O N N E C T B F P A
F L C C O X D D I V I N G U M C N F M Z
W Z A C L J P I A Z T N O K J A I E O I
I W E C O N C E N T R A T I O N W K C V
E K R G J R D P R G S A W M Y U P H Y B
U E W E Z N D J D I V I P E O P L E D D
M S J Y E G K I N N E R H H S I R U O N
T U L V F Q W T N C M N V D C O E R B L
Y J S O A X B S J G B T C Q D W M Q F U
P C R S K C M H L W B V T E Y U M E G F
Q O J L W M L J P K Y G N I A R B B G H
```

Solution on page 168

EMBRACE PLEASANT SENSATIONS

Do you **love** the feel of **sand** between your toes? Do you feel **luxurious** when you lie down on a really soft **carpet**? Do you have a **silk** robe or particularly soft T-shirt to wear when you want to feel **pampered** and **comfortable**?

If none of these **sensations** float your **boat**, there are **probably** some others you love to feel. Whether it's **feeling** something soft, **smooth**, or silky against your skin; **enjoying** the **shivery** sensation you get from a small **breeze**; or **warming** your hands in front of a **fire**, reveling in **pleasant** sensations is one of the best parts of life.

To **parlay** this **fact** into greater **gratitude** for your **body**, commit to **embracing** and enjoying these pleasant sensations—**really** enjoying them, **rather** than simply noting them and **moving** on.

While you enjoy **whatever** sensation you have **chosen**, be **mindful** of the **experience**. Thank your body for its **ability** to feel the silky **rippling** of water, the **nerves** in your skin that **respond** to a **gentle** touch, and the **muscles** that **relax** and drop all the stress they hold when **massaged**.

Practice this **exercise** regularly to stay **thankful** for your body and its **amazing** ability to feel all of these **wonderful** sensations.

```
S Z U G A G E K S A N W H A T E V E R W
E N R K Q R N U Y A L R A P C P T I U L
L C S A T P E I B D N V N R E O P H H R
C H I H W R R L Z R O D C V M P H T J O
S D L T D O V E A A W B A K L I C P F B
U N K O C B E R H X M O N I Z A N N P P
M H D O O A S E H T H A N K F U L G T G
B G H M M B R S Z T A G M D W L P E T F
C O O S F L Q P C E G R A G E Y P J E K
R M D S O Y B O O V E E S I C R E X E L
E X P E R I E N C E N R G G A E F S K U
A X G B T W V D D G G G B C Q V F U S F
L D E G A S S A M T N A R V N I E O L D
L L T C B Z F D N I I I S A R H E I E N
Y U A V L E C A C L V Z Y E T S C R L I
C H O S E N S A T I O N S O Y I E U L M
G Q B L C A R R M J M V M Z J P T X X W
M Y I W E B A H D I W R E Y M N E U L Z
V N J L M C H Y T I L I B A B K E L D D
G O P E L T N E G L X P P O R N T S N E
```

Solution on page 168

OUTDOOR MEDITATION

Nature is the **perfect** route to **meditation** and present-moment **awareness**. By stepping **outdoors** you **surround** yourself with nature's **life force**, which is the same **energy** that runs inside of you. Find **activities** to do that you would **enjoy** outside. There is so much **variety** in nature that you won't get **bored** even if you take **regular** walks along the same **streets**. The sky looks **different** at **sunrise**, midday, sunset, midnight, and the hours in **between**.

Take a **break** from your screens on the **weekend** to go outside and watch cloud **formations**, find **shadows** cast by the sun, or stand in the **rain** and listen to it bounce off your **umbrella**. At **night**, look for **constellations** if the sky is clear. When the **moon** is getting **fuller**, sit outside and **bathe** in the moonlight in the same way you bathe in the sun. **Connecting** to the life force of nature **strengthens** the life force in **you**.

```
N X W D V C R A K Q U U J A U P U U I N
P B H N A W E E K E N D K E Z S T B I E
Y L K U R S E S U L M C Z B U W R G I N
I Y E O I A C P Z Y G R E N E E H I O Y
P Y G R E L R O C M E D I T A T I O N J
S Z N R T L O B C F J T T K C B W O U S
B U M U Y E F J O O T G R O T I O E T Y
S U O S T R E N G T H E N S I M K R E W
A V Z Y Y B F A Z O G S S E V L E Z E N
G Z S N H M I Z Z U T S Z U I E Y S A D
O T E W I U L X L E E N F L T J O R W S
L C C R O Y I A L N J O N S I T J O T I
E S X X U D R L E G N I T C E N N O C H
M W U W A T A R Y X A T V E S R E D E K
F A J W I T A H S R U A B X J Y S T F Y
Q N D M I W P N S M D M D A I W E U R P
X L K O A C D I F F E R E N T K X O E W
Y Y N N I K O V G A R O O X V H F T P K
H S M E V I R E L L U F Q I E P E B J R
Z J E K A I Z S O K M Q V R U D B P R J
```

Solution on page 169

SAVOR THE LITTLE MOMENTS

When you stop to **think** about it, life **really** is all about the **small** stuff. You shouldn't **sweat** the small **stuff**, but you also shouldn't **dismiss** it entirely! It's the **little** things that **matter** most, in the grand **scheme** of things.

If you **appreciate** all the little **moments** and find **joy** in the less **exciting** or **impactful** parts of your day, you will **experience** more **happiness** than if you simply **float** through your day, unmindful of the **positive** moments **happening** all around you.

To **cultivate** more **gratitude** for others, focus on savoring the little moments with them. **Make** an **effort** to **notice** the small things, the **quirks**, and the **kind** words that often go unnoticed. **Seek** out these things when you share a **quiet** moment with your **loved** one or when they don't **realize** you're watching.

For **example**, many **parents** know exactly how to **savor** the little moments because they do this all the time with their **young** children. When it **seems** like they grow up **faster** than should be **possible**, it's **important** to take mental **snapshots** and **maximize** your joy in the experience as it unfolds.

Try paying **extra** attention to the little moments with your loved ones, and be **ready** to **surrender** completely to the experience. When you do, you'll experience a **rush** of love and appreciation for **them**.

```
Y S N P J E Y S A R E A L I Z E D Y W W
U K S F Q C C G C N E V I T I S O P C L
L G A X P J J N N U N D R F Q B B V U O
F Q R U S H W F E I L G N U O Y Y F V S
U L F A M E X X U I N T J E B Q T S E H
V F O G T G C N W U R E I M R C D E P B
W R A A Q I S E T B D E P V A R K E P H
H N B H T E T A I C E R P P A T U M S M
B L Q I L I O U P X K K M X A T T S D S
D F N X C M H O D Z M I D Z E H E E A Z
X G S S I M S I D E M N N E R N N V R M
N F M U B S P K H W S O Z D I E O I E K
V B A I I G A T R C S I M P O R T A N T
W E L B F B N R H I M K P E A K I S O R
K R L G F P S E E I U A N F N R C A A O
L E O T U V M E X A H Q U I E T E S G F
J A V J T E X A M P L E J Q H X S N E F
G D E Z S I M U V M I L E A T T O K T E
C Y D G S R L O O U J O Y R L T A E W S
S L W A B H S T X W R F A L W M D B F I
```

Solution on page 169

LISTEN CAREFULLY

If you **talk** often, **rapidly**, or loudly, your **throat** chakra might be **excessive**. One of the **ways** to **calm** your **energy** down is to set an **intention** to **listen** more often and more **carefully**. **Reassure** yourself that you **will** get your turn to talk, if not **today**, then next time. With an excessive throat **chakra**, you **might** feel you **need** to keep talking to be **heard** and to feel connected. Know that listening will **help** you feel connected. If you **truly** listen to another **person**, you are **witnessing** something **sacred**: a **connection** between two people. It's a **miracle** to be in these **bodies** with these **abilities** to talk, listen, **understand**, and **respond**. And each of us has their own **language**. Even if you **speak** to **someone** who speaks the same **literal** language, often the same **words** will land **differently** for different people. When listening to someone, truly listen.

```
J A U M I G H T F L W Q R F A V U G Z I
T H X O O E N E E D Y I Q I Z O D J F Q
E N S R A N O W H M D S T D G K G L T S
S A C R E D I N O I T C E N N O C A V D
V Q D T V E T Y F E V J A A E N V R S E
D W S I I S N F T H R O A T R S Q E F L
R I S G S O E O T M U S C S U K S T J S
L C E Y S R T I E T V A D R S A D I L L
E X X R E N N R T M A R Y E S E E L N L
O Z E N C M I R Q I O L Q D A P I I A G
Z P T F X Y E Q F W L S K N E S G D T Z
R L B I E S L F F U L I V U R N I R O V
Y F A I P G C D F H I Q B G R Y E J T B
B O O O O Z A E I R W C H A K R A R Q W
R N N H U U R U X P L E H R J A U D G H
F D V P Y A I O G N A Q T S J L K B O Y
D E H C C R M O K N G R G Q Y H Y V R T
D F T C L L D X I D A K L R X A B O C K
J O O D A J R H M K U L G R W E W N L C
D J R C O Y M P J P I M S C N D E M H S
```

Solution on page 169

RELEASE THE PAST AND APPRECIATE THE PRESENT

You can **never** go back to **previous** moments or past **events**. Once you have **moved** through them, they are **forever** gone. Whatever is in the **past** that haunts you or **makes** you sad or fearful **necessarily** stays there. It **cannot** be **undone**. If some past event or **encounter** still **bothers** you, do what you can to **process** through it and let it go. You **alone** give it the **power** it has over you. **Release** it and instead **focus** on the **present** moment. Be **mindful** right now of **where** you are, who you are, and **what** you are **doing**. Paying **attention** to and being **fully** present in each **moment** of your life means you **truly** will be "**showing** up for your life." That is the way to **happiness**.

```
G A X N U I O T F M Z A B K D X X O O M
F N J T R L J Q O U P L L M V R T L B F
Y A I I Q O U N R N L Z H L D W J M E R
O A C O J N V D E P N L D O K I J Z M W
E Q T V D S F X V C R A Y I T M I C S T
Q U G O E Y E N E G E A C U S T F A A H
B R N T B U P C R N T S E K A M O S L Y
Z E G H M V Z H D F N Z S H P J A O L Y
R N S U R M I N D F U L W A E N P M R P
X O B A X W Q R E W O P Y T R O J D W T
V L P B E H Y I S Y C P R E V I O U S B
B A L W K L Z Y W S N S X E P T L J U K
A K B S U M E M O V E D R M G N D Y C Q
B Q L R B A P R E S E N T E R E H W O T
D V T W Y D M T R Z H F I Q H T T H F N
E J F M H K X S S E C O R P S T N E V E
F T N A J P S Z I P V H W D P A O O F M
N I O W V M Q O I T X E I I B A H B N O
Q C V J P W H A A Q M U N U N D H L P M
P I S Y R Z Y E M V V P X C P G V D X Y
```

Solution on page 170

DESIGNATE ONE CORNER OF YOUR HOME AS SACRED SPACE

Create an **area** in your **home** that can serve as a **sanctuary** for **yoga**, prayer, writing in your **journal**, sipping tea, **reading**, and **reflecting**. Make your sacred space **private**. Add a **screen**, a large **plant**, a **curtain**, or something that **defines** and **separates** that **space** from the rest of the **house**. Add a small **table** to hold your **spiritual** texts, **sacred** objects, **candles**, **incense**, holy oil, or **prayer beads**. A **window** or door with a view of a **lake** or **garden** is an added **bonus**. **Otherwise** hang a piece of silk, a **batik**, or spiritual art. **Regularly** retreat to your sanctuary to **reconnect** with your own **inner** joy.

```
U V D K B T B D X W O D N I W L N S X X
B Q F N I Y T B B S S E E G U T V M R W
F R S H S R P M Z P A X X F M T M E K S
U X G Y S Z B G W I C G Y H I J N X E G
U T D M D W B J N R R G O L A N R U O J
Z L R G Q C R P L I E H J Y I J E K V B
F O E K Q S T X Y T D C A N D L E S X G
A X F Y L Y N N R U A A U H O M E P X G
P M Y U P P C N A A R V E P O T R C V M
N T B G N I T C E L F E R R A E U H Y O
T L W Y Q B Q R J O P A G R C R E A T E
V F X S F T E H Z O Y R A U T C N A S N
R O T H E R W I S E O P S A L K L C E D
Z X M I E S H X R R E U I Y K A P E P S
T A Z N L K E B O S N N N K K L R U J E
K W V C T C E N N O C E R S I C I L E B
L R W E C A S K B S A D L K S T V C Y P
V J E N D J U L A Q I R O B B V A P A Q
X V Y S H G O A P L G A E K A P T B C F
F D B E I N H E L W V G E A S T E Q K K
```

Solution on page 170

COMMITTING TO ANOTHER

Love is a **wonderful** roller-coaster **ride** in life. You are extremely **fortunate** if you find **someone** to **share** your life with in a **committed** relationship. **More** than in most other **kinds** of **relationships**, the **propensity** for suffering here **rears** its head. Love **often** means the **possibility** of suffering. **Practicing** Zen and mindfulness in your love relationships does not **mean** that your love **life** will be suffering-free and **joyous** twenty-four hours a day, **seven** days a week. But practicing **Zen** and mindfulness in your love life does mean that you **accept** the suffering and remain openhearted and **compassionate**. You sit, and you sit **whether** you suffer or not.

Finding another to share your life with, **however**, does not mean that you have **found** your **missing** half. You **already** have **everything** you need, and **perhaps** love is just a nice **addition**. No one else can make you **whole**. You are already whole. No one else can **give** you **anything** you don't already have, and if you are **looking** outside yourself for **completion**, you are **indeed** setting **yourself** up for suffering.

```
A Z Z S D T X V Y M P F H O W E V E R E
A I Q Y M K M Y V F O U H B D Y T E V G
U H H B U I S S P A H R E P Z A H O N T
F C M W P H Y E P N W M E A N T L I F E
O K B H A A E O V I F N V O E F C W C S
O W Y O C T L K U E H E I H Y I T O K E
V R Q C V J O R Y R N S W H T F M N D V
A N E T F O H C E O S I N C I P L D Z I
D P G N G Y W O E A A E A O L D T E E G
T A V A L O N M P D D R L E I Y S R N N
D H B N X U O M D X P Y T F B T A F C I
X W I Y U S O I I R V I U O I H A U A H
A G O T K C T T U F O U N D S X L L R T
C H N H W I Z T O N J H R H S N L L E Y
W U B I O M N E T A N U T R O F O I A R
P Q J N D H P D Y T I S N E P O R P R E
M L P G Q N R O S A R O R N K C N J S V
W C W E Y N I M J T Q G N I S S I M D E
N C R G J M D F X B X I N D E E D C S M
K C E I G B E N N O P G E I Q A Z Z K K
```

Solution on page 170

HAVE A CONVERSATION WITH YOUR PAST SELF

You've **probably** seen one of those **movies** where, through the **magic** of **time travel** or some **supernatural** force, a **character** is able to share a quick **message** with his or her past self.

Unfortunately, we do not have the **technology** necessary for such a **conversation**! What we do have is the **ability** to think back on our old **selves** and **connect** them to our **present** self. When you have a little **spare** time and you're feeling **centered** and **ready**, think back to an **important** moment in your life. It should be at **least** a few **years** past and during a time of indecision, confusion, or **stress**. **Visualize** this version of yourself in **detail**—what is this **version** dealing with in this **moment**?

Once you have a **clear** image in mind, **think** about what you want to tell this **former** version of you. **Consider** what would have **pleased** that version to **know** about the **future**; for **instance**, you may want to **reassure** your former self that they are **making** a good **decision** that will **positively** affect **events** to come.

After you **share** your message with your former self, think about how you got from **there** to here. Send some **gratitude** toward your past self, and **extend** it to your **current** self as well. Be **thankful** for what you've **experienced**, because it **brought** you to where you are now.

```
C H L R D J I O S R P T Y X D L S X S N
I U B T R L E V A R T E M I T S P O L S
G K G H S S A B I L I T Y Y D I A F T E
A N O I T A S R E V N O C P W O R N X B
M O S H A R E V U R C F U T U R E T B R
A F L V X X D L L T X U X W N V E P E E
K R O E A O V I S U A L I Z E N R D R A
I K R R E X P E R I E N C E D E I E G S
N M N S M A A N R A C J R E S S H R L S
G E P I S E C Y B S H K J E N T A P R U
F S P O H E R G N S A Y N O P T C T I R
M S E N R T V O M E R T C O I U E N I E
N A C I M T I L C R A A S T W J S R J F
N G U X V S A O E T C I U D H T M M E Y
W E R M I O N N E S T D J R A G R D H D
Y D R C G N M H T I E L C N A F U F F A
E R E B E L F C V Y R A C T N E M O M E
R D N C S R A E Y P L E A S E D L S R R
D E T A I L L T H A N K F U L J L C P B
O L R V Z Y L B A B O R P H G F Q H U G
```

Solution on page 171

SO HUM MEDITATION

One of the **simplest** and most **profound** mantras is "**So Hum**"—"I am that I am." **Meditating** on this simple **phrase**, you **penetrate** your **layers** of **protection** and self-criticism. As you **repeat** "So Hum" over and **over**, you bring your **awareness** to who you are at the **core**. The **quiet**, still **place**. You discover simply that you exist, that you are.

Sit in a **comfortable** meditation **posture**. Feel your **sitting** bones rooted **solidly**. Sit up with a **steady** spine, without trying to **straighten** out the **natural** curves. Make **sure** that the top of your head is **parallel** to the **ceiling**, with the back of your neck long. Take a deep **inhale** in, and let out a long **exhale**. Take two more deep **breaths**, making the exhale **longer** than the inhale. **Close** your eyes and **bring** your hands into **prayer** position at the **Anahata chakra** (a.k.a. the heart chakra). As you breathe in, **imagine** the **syllable** "So," and as you breathe out, imagine the syllable "Hum." Do this **several** times. As you do this, make sure your **jaw** is relaxed. Begin to feel your **entire** body **relaxing** into this **mantra**.

Place your **hands**, one on top of the **other**, at your **sacral** chakra. Inhale **deeply**, and on the exhale, **chant** "So Hum." It doesn't **matter** what **musical** note you chant. Chant a few times with your hands and **attention** at your sacral chakra, which is the chakra that helps you **flow** through life and **connects** you to pleasure. Take pleasure in the simplicity and **vastness** of this mantra: "I am that I am. So Hum."

```
R N E L A H X E R U S M Q O I L O C X N
O E S H T A E R B S O H U M E A S W A L
J K T A T D N S E V E R A L O Y X T F V
Y W E N E C E I L I N G A E J E U X U E
R S A D N P T W K T I H C J L R O V E R
L P D S T L H A P N N A X F A S N R N C
Q H Y F I L G C E I L A V L C E U R T D
I R B G O C I U N P Z V H A I T X W I D
X A C N N S A E E Q E W T C S G N I R B
P S G I P I R L T T C R O O U T F G E M
K E O T H M T B R X E O P D M E N L C N
R L H T E P S A A C S L N M A I K E O Z
L E M I H L R T T S S S B N X U R I S W
E I Y S T E D R E I C O E A E Q T W B S
L R N A T S R O J P D O L N L C C J M A
L W Z T R T Z F F F E E R I E L T V A C
A J A W U P E M B C R S M T D R Y S N R
R M D N U O F O R P O V O W P L A S T A
A N A H A T A C H A K R A L V S Y W R L
P T N C V F L P Y L P E E D C U P Y A J
```

Solution on page 171

YOU COMMUNICATE WITH THE UNIVERSE

You are not **separate** from the **earth**. With every **inhale** and **exhale** you are **plugging** in to the same **energy** that **sustains** the **entire** Universe. The **healthy** food you eat and the **water** you **drink** come from **nature**. You **receive** your energy and physical **sustenance** from the earth, which **means** your **vibrations** and needs are **compatible** with the vibrations and **gifts** of the earth. The **fuel** of the earth is fuel for your **physical** body. You **thrive** when you **exist** in **harmony** with nature. Just as your physical body is compatible with earth's **produce**, on an energetic **level** your vibrations are compatible with the **other** vibrations in the **Universe**. This includes the vibrations of **plants**, animals, and water. Your vibrations **resonate** outward into the Universe, and the Universe **answers** your **request**. According to the **Law of Attraction**, the Universe works to **match** the vibrations you **send** out, bringing your **desires** into being as soon as **seven** seconds after you feel the desire. Your **task**, after putting your desires out there, is to be **receptive**.

```
C V D N O K M F S M G N I G G U L P L M
V D K J L T Z B P R L Y H T L A E H L P
G P M A I N H A L E E B U O C F U E L G
M F H S A U F E X X M W W I L S V C I X
M N W R R D Y H R C B W S A K E X I S T
O W E F F H A R M O N Y W N L V S V I E
W F M V C L E M Q M H O B V A I R D Q Z
C U F D E Q H G Z P F N A T U R E E H G
L Y L A U S H I S A B N H T E H S S A W
V F S E V V W F T T M R J C N T O I F A
I M S I T H I T N I S E N D P D N R U D
B T U L N M R S A B I A Z J C R A E Z B
R H S H E A X M L L N T W R K R T S L Q
A I T H C T S H P E V I T P E C E R T G
T S A T U C X E T A R A P E S C M E R A
I A I G D H Q S N R S E R I T N E V U X
O O N T O R U M K E A I I P T K A I M Y
N W S L R S I R Z M R E T A W X N N V M
S V S O P R R N Y Z F G S X Q E S U Q E
S Y A M V E L V K V F K Y I M O Y G X H
```

Solution on page 171

THE GIFT OF IMAGINATION

Imagination is the **best** way to come up with new **ideas** for your life. Let your imagination go. There's no **risk** in imagining what you **would** like to do or have in your **life**. What have you **wanted** to do since you were **young**? Or, what have you **heard** of others doing **recently** that you **wish** you could do? Is there an **adventure** or a **relaxation** break you're **interested** in taking, even if not this **year**? Even if it seems like it would take a **miracle** for your **dreams** to happen, write your **answers** onto a **sheet** of paper. On another piece of **paper**, write down all the **thoughts** that are coming up, telling you **reasons** why you cannot have or do those things. Get the negative thoughts out of your **system**. Now, on the back of the **first** page that has your wish list, write down how you could **literally** make them **happen**. What **steps** would you need to take? Even if they seem **unrealistic**, write them down. When a **negative** thought comes up, write that on the **other** piece of paper that has your negative thoughts on it.

At the end of this **exercise**, burn or **throw** away the negative thoughts and reread the wish list. **Keep** that in your **daily** planner or in your **purse**. Just let it ride along with you throughout your days. When you have the **energy** and time to **work** with it more, take it out **again** and start doing the steps. **Until** then, though, let your wish list just **hang** out with you as you go about your daily life. Something **magical** might **eventually** happen. Taking the **time** to let your imagination flow **freely** helps **open** you up to your dreams of what you want and **need** in your life. **Each** of us needs rest time, play time, and **fulfillment**. Allow your imagination to tell you what your **heart** desires. **Acknowledge** it, write it down, **nurture** it.

```
N K J G Y V D T I M E V I T A G E N G W
R R U W S E B P K X X L M I R A C L E P
X O R I L B A G Q H S M A E R D N I N E
F W T S W P W R N O T L G C M H E T E M
D L I H E M O S S U H H I P I P P N R G
K S I R E X H A W Z O V N T K G P U G V
N U R T U R E R M L U Y A L E N A I Y T
Q V T L F D Y R R I G W T C U R H M A T
Q S S G I D P L C B H L I I W N A G U B
W O R H T T E N L I T I O T D O A L J K
S T B E S O E T U A S F N S G I U X L S
D T Y R W P K Y S J U E J I N T Z L F Y
V E I U O S L G C E M T Y L I A D I D S
Q F T T R T N H S L R G N A H X B E S T
D E E N N I E A L A W E R E Y A H C A E
B T G E A A Z I E K Z B T R V L Y R S M
C E C V R W F H R E A S O N S E E R H X
O E G D E L W O N K C A V U I R U E J T
R H U A U C B L L G K D S T E P S J R E
I S D F U V U F S D W B M T W Z X W U F
```

Solution on page 172

A NEW HABIT BEGINS WITH INTENTION AND RESOLVE

Choose a **healthy** new habit like **drinking** a glass of **water** first thing in the **morning** instead of **reaching** for a **caffeinated** beverage. **Experts** say it takes twenty-one days or longer to break a **habit** or form a new one. For **spiritual** seekers, it's **worth** noting that **Eastern** and **Western** wisdom **teachers** suggest **aligning** your personal **willpower** with that of the **Divine** and using **faith** and determination to stay the **course**.

1. **Stand** with your **hands** folded in **prayer** and set your **intention**.

2. Leave your **palms** slightly apart so the **energy** of the bad habit can **flow** away.

3. **Lower** your palms into **open** cups at your **waist** to receive the energies available in the **Universe** to help you establish the healthy habit.

4. **Close** your eyes. **Adopt** the **Buddhist** approach of **resisting** the temptation to **think**, feel, or do what is not **beneficial** and healthy.

5. **Relax** and summon your **consciousness** and **dynamic** will.

6. Mentally **affirm** your desire to align your willpower with the will and power of the **Creator**.

7. **Focus** your **thoughts** on letting go of the old habit. **Release** it.

8. Affirm your **desire** and intention to make the new habit a part of your daily **regimen**.

9. Be faithful in your **resolve**.

10. **Reinforce** your intention throughout the day with affirmations, **reminder** notes, and **images** associated with your new habit.

```
O S O K T O X A J K D H E V L O S E R Q
R Q H H C K A F L I D R E T A W X T A N
G E I L Z B H F V X J R P S O P E N R R
S N L V R E S I S T I N G F E C L Z E E
K E I A E N N R S S G E S R U O C G L G
A R U K X E Z M E H S N T P O D A Y E I
Q G W M N F C D G T T S I H D D U B A M
S Y D V M I M K A R R M U N I V E R S E
F D S E M C R N M O L P O P G S A T E N
G G N A T I D D I W F A A R O I P I T S
Q U N A V A I L A B L E U L N V L B H W
R Y P S H L N W R G R H C T M I F A O I
D H F R E D N I M E R O E R I S N H U L
D P W E A O R E E N A N T A O R Z G G L
L W J H F Y A E R F T C H A L F I A H P
V O H C W S E N S I F B H F E T N P T O
C W W A T T Z R O O H A A I W R H I S W
B W I E S S E N S U O I C S N O C Y E E
D S R T R P M T Y T T H L Z O G L Z W R
T N R E T S E W Q H S U C O F T J F R C
```

Solution on page 172

FIVE PURIFICATION BREATHS

The **exercise** that **prepares** the **Sufi** practitioner for **rhythmic** breathing is the five **purifications** of the **soul**. The **universal** elements are the **focal** points of **earth**, water, **fire**, and **air**. Begin at **sunrise** if possible, when the **elements** are at their **peak**. Stand **upright**.

    Breathe slowly and **deeply**, keeping in mind the **energy** of the earth. **Visualize** it as the **color** yellow, entering your body as you **inhale** through the **nose**. The earth element travels **upward** from the **ground** through your **spine** to your **crown**. As it does so, the earth **filters** out all **impurities**. It returns to the ground when you **exhale** through the nose. **Repeat** this four more times (a total of five).

    Breathe **slowly** and deeply, keeping in **mind** the energy of **water**. Visualize it as the color **green**, entering your nose as you inhale. The water element moves upward from the **stomach**, through your spine to your crown. As it **does** so, the **liquid** washes away all impurities. It **exits** from your stomach when you exhale through the **mouth**. Repeat this **four** more times (a total of five).

    Breathe slowly and deeply, **keeping** in mind the energy of fire. Visualize it as the color **red**, entering your body through your **heart** as you inhale. The fire element moves upward to your crown. As it does so, the fire **burns** away all impurities. It exits from your heart when you exhale through the nose. Repeat this four more times (a total of **five**).

    Breathe slowly and deeply, keeping in mind the energy of air. Visualize it as the color **blue**, **entering** your body through all of your **pores** as you inhale. The air element moves through all the **organs** and tissues, **blowing** away all the impurities. It exits through the pores when you exhale through your mouth. Repeat this four more **times** (a total of five).

```
T W Z B F J Q C Z R D B E E V H Y H N G
U L F K P S O W P I L A S G Z U I M Q Y
A T C H H L M R U K L I R N U P F W N Q
O V I T O O A Q G A S E O D R G U W A Z
K E L R B W I C F A E S I R N U S Y S Y
V W H A A L U A O N N B O I L E B G M S
G V K E Q Y O N Z F D S R E T L I F W G
R R F A M D M W I W P E L E M E N T S N
O J W S E R O P I V T J A U A F D N I M
U Z W L D G U U J N E T O L W T O E D J
N S D V E P T S E A G R U B A I H U R V
D O T R I R H Y E F R O S E T G N E R T
Y E S I A S H K R I S H C A M O T S U H
G L E E X W U E U R T R C Y L I K Z P G
U A H P R E P A R E S I W M N N W O R C
R H L K L E N U L J F A R H Y T H M I C
U X F C A Y T E F I V E A U L B W O G F
A E W T Z E E A R E Z L Q S P I N E H V
K K U X O A P U W G E E H S E M I T T U
P L J G N I P E E K Y E X E R C I S E N
```

Solution on page 172

COUNT YOUR BLESSINGS
WHEN YOU WAKE UP

Start your **day** on the right side of the bed by **counting** your **blessings** the **moment** you **wake** up. Morning may not be your **favorite** time, but it's a **great** time to **practice** a little **gratitude** and set yourself up for a **good** day.

The moment you wake up, as **soon** as you **turn** off your **alarm**, think of at **least** five or six **things** you're grateful for **right** now. If you can, try to practice this **exercise** before you **even** open your **eyes**. When you count your blessings at such a **unique** and **vulnerable** time, you often come up with some **interesting**, silly, and **profound** blessings. For **example**, you **might** be **immediately** grateful that it's **summer** because it's **light** out when you wake up, **rather** than dark and dreary. You might **find** yourself being **thankful** that you live **just** down the street from your favorite **coffee** shop, or **perhaps** you'll be **filled** with **love** and thankfulness for your **significant** other **lying** beside you in bed.

Whatever it is you're grateful for in the morning, you can be **sure** that it's **honest** and **authentically** you. If you're the **kind** of **person** who wakes with **little** idea of your plans for the day—or even what your own **name** is—you might want to set a **reminder** on your **phone** or just put a **sticky** note where you'll see it right **away**.

```
S U F L O O J V L B V E N O H P Y H X X
E B S K A Y T S A E L U E W E S O Y T U
Q X P S W S C O L D N E L R A N Y N S L
C Y A D Q Q A O F E S R S N E M A N U U
N J H M T U R N V I C O E S E C J F Q U
R D R E P S E E C F N O T M I R K R F N
K I E M L L V R D Z D D U F M N A T F I
H Q P M O M E N T N Q F I N A U G B D Q
O W X M B X T M I U I N S H T O S S L U
A X S Y E D A K G L G M T H O I L O V E
F T E K L H H P L I N B E D W K N T J T
C F H C Y N W E S B I N Y R G S I G U I
B J X I I S D Y L E T A I D E M M I R R
C S H T N T L M F I S O X M B S V T I O
V U H S G G C I C G E D U T I T A R G V
P R E S S K S A G P R E I T G G R E H A
T E P K G T L S R H E U F O U R H H T F
S Y A W A L A R M P T C P F E K E T Z K
D E M S Y W Z R F D N U O F O R P A P N
T S U J R V N F T L I T T L E C W R T U
```

Solution on page 173

MAKE A TEN-POINT LIST OF WHAT'S REALLY IMPORTANT TO YOU

Millions of **people** live their **lives** without a sense of **direction**. Unless you know what is really **important** to you and what you **want** out of life, how are you **going** to know where you are going, how to get what you want, and what your life **purpose** is? **Think** of ten **things** that are **really** important to you; for **example**, family **unity**. Then make each **item** as **specific** as possible. Instead of **family** unity, maybe you really mean **eating** meals **together**, working on the **chores** together, or **praying** together. **Refine** the ten things on your **list** until you **know** exactly what is of **primary** importance to **you**. These are the things that will make you **happiest**. Knowing what they are can **help** you make better **choices** in your **personal** life **journey**.

```
B E D E R G X M O J Z I Y W P M I Q Z D
Q I X P B Z S X I Q N R E H T E G O T F
C E R Y K S L V V W D L A N O S R E P T
F A C L N B M S F E L P M A X E L E L Z
X H R Y I M E S D G P U R E J C B E V S
O Q B U H V C H O I C E S I T Z F E W A
O G L Q T J E Z E P R T I E M I F Y O U
F Q T N H L A S Y H X E E Y N A A C N Z
R S G N I H T F L S G K C F H S R I K F
K Y V K A J I S I M P O R T A N T Y O G
S Y F D R W N W M I C E D M I Y J N S C
U R M Z R Z G Y A L N H C E S O P R U P
G H W Z C B R R F L J P O I U K N G O K
G I O C N O Y L H I E G Q R F P O Q L H
W V V E P E L Z P O R N N K E I Q H E D
J F B W H K L T P N M E J I N S C K B M
Y J V L O B A L H S Y J F G Y S O M L J
A Q O O B Z E W Z R O T S I L A L C V J
P S E E M Q R D D Z U X O N N M R E E N
K Q S F D G P P H J D I V P L E H P I A
```

Solution on page 173

CREATE A NEW TRADITION WITH YOUR FAMILY

__Brainstorm__ with your __children__ and __spouse__ about making a new __family__ tradition. Perhaps something __wonderful__ and __spontaneous__ occurred as you were __preparing__ to leave for __summer__ vacation, the __night__ before __Thanksgiving__, the __afternoon__ of the first __snowfall__, or on the way to the __pumpkin__ patch. Or __maybe__ you had a __pillow__ fight that ended with __everyone__ making __popcorn__, s'mores, and watching old __movies__ in their __pajamas__...if it still __evokes__ powerful __memories__ for all of you, make it a __tradition__. Other __ideas__ might include an annual family cleaning day (when everyone __pitches__ in to __tackle__ the mess in the garage, __basement__, or attic), an __annual__ family fun day (let a child __choose__ what the family does for the day, even if it's bug hunting), or an annual plant-a-garden day. According to Dr. G. Scott Wooding, bestselling author and __leading__ Canadian __authority__ on parenting __teenagers__, traditions help to __determine__ family __boundaries__ and help children feel more __secure__ by giving them a __sense__ of belonging to a clearly __defined__ unit.

```
F U N G X V B E X S X E E V O K E S X X
A C Q Z P H Z S H C S A S U M M E R B P
M F Y H P N M N F J N A V I L H N E U U
S A E D I E V E V N S E F E C G W M O M
N M Y B P W O S U O E N A T N O P S P O
V I B B C V O A Q M A D I I E K J L R V
Z L L B E B L L E E I P V J I R T Y I I
W Y U E Z V B M L N H I H N T A N Z N E
T S V F R F O R G I G E P E B N F O N S
S R W N R R U J A S P A J A M A S O O S
C E H J I E N P K I F Y S L H Z Y A I N
S G C E D P D N R Q N E K C H R U Z T O
P A S U H M A N A E M S H Y E T F A I W
B N M W R H R S O E P I T V H N I H D F
B E O F T E I E N W L A E O Q T U L A A
Z E N I M R E T E D M S R N R P K O R L
Z T S P O U S E R W O I N I C M W U T L
H M D E N I F E D O T J U G N E H B C A
P O P C O R N R H Y T Y D H M G H P K O
Z Q D S Y T A C K L E M W T Y C E E P A
```

Solution on page 173

WALKING THE LABYRINTH

The **labyrinth** is a **medieval** devotion that has been **revived** in recent **decades**. An **intricate** geometrical **pattern** originally **built** into the floor of a **cathedral**, the labyrinth **allows** the **faithful** to make a **metaphorical** pilgrimage to **Jerusalem** without leaving **home**. The **center** of the **circular** pattern **represents** Jerusalem, and the **seeker** must reach the center by **means** of the **circuitous** outside pathways. The labyrinth is not a **maze**: The **path** will lead to the center if **followed** long enough, and there are no dead ends or **detours**. **Psychologically**, though, the labyrinth plays on the walker's **expectations**, as the way that **seems** to be close to the center will **often** lead right back to the outer **edge** again.

If **walked** with **intention**, the labyrinth becomes a way of **bodily** prayer. It can become a **complex** form of **introspection**, or it can **simply** be a few **minutes** spent in **silence**. Students of **religion** will find the comparisons to **yogic** yantras and **Tibetan** mandalas to be striking. **Churches** in major **metropolitan** areas will often have a labyrinth available for walking, and **portable** versions, printed on **canvas**, are also **available**. Walking the labyrinth can be a **good** way to mark the **beginning** or end of a **retreat**, prepare for a **worship** service or **meditation** group, or get rid of nagging **distractions** and doubts. This **deceptively** simple, traditional **devotion** will allow you to walk your way to your own center as you walk **through** the labyrinth.

U Y L R S T E O F T E N G O O D R J Y E
N L Q L I I R H X A Q N C A N V A S O L
D L F A M B L W T R I D E W O L L O F B
I A S R P E M E O N E T T H R O U G H A
N C U D L T Z E N R I T H O M E C Z V T
T I O E Y A S I E C S R R F F Q R A S R
E G T H M N G N J I E H Y E U Q I E W O
N O I T C E P S O R T N I B A L C K O P
T L U A B D L A C I R O H P A T E M L G
I O C C E E B U I L T X C B Z L S M L X
O H R J T C J E R U S A L E M M E R A L
N C I K A E S M E E S E T E G D E E V K
O Y C C C P S E H C R U H C I P K P E J
I S N O I T C A R T S I D T E P E R I W
T P R M R I Y L I D O B A P R P R E D A
O A E P T V O M I N U T E S J E X S E L
V T T L N E G N A T I L O P O R T E M K
E H T E I L I J N O I G I L E R L N O E
D E A X J Y C S N A E M T S R U O T E D
A W P Y H R E V I V E D E C A D E S Y C

Solution on page 174

CHAKRA HEALING CAN ILLUMINATE YOUR LIFE PATH

Chakra **healing** can be a huge **support** as you **discover** and **follow** your life's **purpose**. When you do **grounding** practices for the **root chakra** to keep it in **balance**, your **body** will feel grounded. When the body feels grounded, your **mind** calms down. As you move up the chakras and balance the **sacral** chakra, you **enliven** your **ability** to go with the **flow**. You **might** need to **accept** some **upcoming** change, and this **helps** you **adapt**. Moving up to the **solar plexus** chakra, you **stoke** the fire of will, self-esteem, and **stamina**. Healing the **heart** chakra will help you in your **connections** with others; **perhaps** they'll give **advice** and **wisdom**. A balanced **throat** chakra will help you stay **true** to yourself when **choices** arise. The **third eye** chakra will be your connection to your wisdom. And when you **meditate** on the **crown** chakra you'll **experience** the **calm** feeling of **oneness** that **restores** you on this **journey**.

```
W E F F Q O J T T V P E S T O K E S V N
B G D E E G H P Z H B J X T P E C C A Z
A B S G N I L A E H R E Z P A A W S F M
X R M H P L Y D A L C O N I J M O G I Q
T Y K F E F I A Y E V L A B I L I T Y E
H R C A R G T V I M E D I T A T E N L B
Q E O E H V N A E C N E I R E P X E A N
D R L P A C F I X N I U P C O M I N G O
A K U P P D T Q D J R L D E G J X J G N
P H I F S U C O N N E C T I O N S F R H
S U L E M H S R O X U H Y R S E Y D O B
W H H C O J W S U R I O F C R C M G N Y
G B Y I A I Z S O R A Z R O A N O I E T
K C C V S L A E D Q W E T G L A W V N Y
X E V D O D M E N K Q S W D S L W K E D
S A O A K H Y O X W E O Y A V A O N S R
B M I R T E H H E R O P C D L B R W S P
J D Q P O A X U C D S R T N W U G T N C
O F Q D S R R K J G A U C W O L F A I O
Q M I G H T D V L L I P S J L G E U D B
```

Solution on page 174

MEDITATE WITH CRYSTALS FOR HEALING

Place a **crystal** in your **nondominant** hand. **Meditate** on the crystal, its healing **power**, and the **intention** you want to **infuse** in it. Hold the crystal in your **hand**, and then move your hand **toward** the area of your body for **healing** to occur. **Hold** it there, with the crystal **against** your body, and meditate on its healing **energy**. On each **exhale**, envision the crystal **drawing** negative energy out. On each **inhale**, imagine the **body** absorbing the crystal's healing energy.

If you **want** to do this **lying** down, you can lay the crystals on your body and meditate with them **there** while you lie down. Some say that the **less** you **touch** the crystals the **better**; that way their energy remains **purely** their own. **Others** say as long as you keep your energy **positive** and on your healing, then your own hands and energy will **enhance** the crystal's **effects**. Try it both **ways** and see which way works **best** for you.

After you've **finished** using the crystals for this **visualization**, take some time for the healing effects to **integrate**. Give yourself a few **moments**, at least, before **resuming** other **activities**. Allow the healing **influence** of the crystals to **sink** in.

```
S D J U E W R B T X K Q Z X L F X F N V
T Y A C K Z F F P I S P L M M C E T W S
O R E Y X C B G O F U B O Y C R L A E Y
Z W T O U P X W W R O M X S V Y Y H R W
U J Y Z N P P A E B E F I N I S H E D U
C K L Z Z J N L R N S G T V S T X M N H
F R G G X T Y B T I E N S D U A I O A Y
R W N N R O P S N N I I P E A L Z V H T
F X E I I L S K X T T L F L L Z J G E Y
W V G M N W Z I G E I A G A I N S T E Q
N A T U K F A G B N V E V H Z S Y A C T
R V L S E E L R N T I H D X A L G Q N O
H F E E E L T U D I T C U E T Z R O A W
G G S R T B A A E O C Q K I I T E C H A
G K S R H D N H T N A N I M O D N O N R
T O I A E S U F N I C L Y I N G E J E D
A P L Q R H O L D I D E T A R G E T N I
X K J Q E Z T C E F F E C T S Q T X H Z
Z P N T H C U O T Y N S M H N E B Y A U
P F Q F G F E I U L T Y D O B Y T B N M
```

Solution on page 174

USE INTENTION TO MANIFEST SOMETHING DESIRED

The **Law of Attraction** is a **philosophical** idea that **asserts** that the **power** of your **thought** is always drawing to you **positive** and negative **people**, objects, **situations**, and **circumstances**. Mind **chatter** goes on **endlessly**, and since the **force** of attraction does not **discriminate** between **good** and bad thoughts, it **makes** sense to keep a positive **state** of mind. **Formulate** a clear **intention** and then **infuse** it with the **belief** that you deserve what you ask for; **trust** that what you ask for, you'll **receive**; and feelings of **confidence**, joy, **expectancy**, and **gratitude**. Use the following **meditation** technique to get started.

....

1. Sit with **eyes** closed.

2. **Visualize** a specific **object** you **desire**.

3. **Mentally** state your intention to **draw** your heart's desire into your life. Be **bold** and **specific** in your declaration. For **example**, if you want a **string** of beads to use for **chanting prayers** or a **mantra**, you might say the following: "I desire to **manifest** a japa mala of 108 **sandalwood** prayer beads from **India** tied with red string, and I am drawing it to me now."

4. **Affirm** you are **deserving** and ready to receive. Make a **space** in your life for the object.

5. **Stoke** a feeling of **jubilation**, feeling as you will when the object **arrives**, not **questioning** when or how it will come.

6. **Know** that a positive **outcome** is always **possible** when you yoke your will-power to the **Unseen** Power at work in the **Universe**.

7. Feel **genuine** gratitude for all that comes to you when you **align** your will with that of the **Creator**.

```
D L O B A I D N I E K O T S R A W A R D
E T Q S D Y E M A N I F E S T M C E E O
S H K L E E L P M A X E C P N E H V W O
I G S W S C M S E K A M N E O N A I O G
R U O N A P N O S P A C E C I T T T P G
E O U N O H Y A C E M E D I T A T I O N
C H A N T I N G T T L T I F N L E S S I
E T E I D L T A W S U D F I E L R O S V
I C Z O O O T A V F M O N C T Y R P I R
V E I P O S T S U R T U O E N P G T B E
E J L A W O F A T T R A C T I O N B L S
M B A S L P E T A N I M I R C S I D E E
A O U S A H D E V R E S E D I B N X E D
N P S E D I U N I V E R S E P C O U S D
T R I R N C T K P F N O I T A L I B U J
R A V T A A I Y X F O R M U L A T E F A
A Y B S S L T I Z G A R R I V E S W N L
B E L I E F A Y C N A T C E P X E O I I
C R E A T O R A F F I R M E N I U N E G
L S T R I N G P E O P L E Y E S Q K L N
```

Solution on page 175

TAKING IN THE COLORS OF THE NATURAL WORLD

Notice the **myriad** ways in **nature** that **color** appears, and use the **vibration** of the **light** from those natural **objects** to **affect** you. For **example**, for **nourishing** your **heart** take a **walk** in the green **spring** grass. For **groundedness** in the **winter**, buy yourself a red **poinsettia**. To **heighten** your **connection** to **spirit**, keep purple **lavender** by your **bedside**. Take time to **look** at these objects, and be **mindful** of what you **surround** yourself with in your home and **office**. Your body **perceives** the vibrations, even if you aren't looking. There's **never** a lack of **inspiration** from nature when it comes to color. **Flowers** come in **spectacular** shapes and colors, and the colors of **animals**, plants, and the sky are **innumerable**. Taking in the vibrations of color will **stimulate** your body if you aren't **completely** energetically closing yourself off.

```
L R U J T V G S R A P E R U T A N X M Q
G T D Z I G E W S I N O T I C E J I S Z
Q N V B R I Q D K E A I T T E S N I O P
S F I T I M C V I Y N Z N G F D W J P I
U P M H P D U V T S C D M Y F L X Z S H
R T E J S X A W P R D O E U A L I T L W
R Q E C Q I A I W X Y E L D H N E N S A
O F E L T L R J R R I R B O N N K G P E
U Q B N K A H U D Y L E J U R U C C R C
N R D V T V C E O X M V M V Y A O A I I
D T S I H E V U I N C E P T F N M R N F
G Z O B A N X J L G R N E D N I P A G F
P N M R E D C T M A H U R E G M L A U O
Y B O A X E X O B A R T C T L A E D B O
L Q P T A R U L W I N T E R I L T J M X
C A T I M H E A R T I W I N G S E X Y R
N E C O P S R E W O L F V Q H C L L G U
J Z Q N L Q W A N F O M E A T O Y L E C
Q H W F E T A L U M I T S S O T L C N U
N Z B R W F I P Z C U B K K B W B A L V
```

Solution on page 175

A VISUAL MEDITATION

View an **image** overall for about five **minutes**, allowing it to "**impress**" on you. Do not seek **detail**; see it as a **whole**. Close your **eyes** and see the **overall** image in your **mind**. If you can't "see" it with your eyes **closed**, open your eyes and **return** to the image once more. For the next **five** minutes, **allow** your **attention** to seek the details of the image. A **constructive** approach is to **begin** at the base (six o'clock **position**) and continue in a **clockwise** direction. You may **notice** colors, **designs**, numbers of **petals** on the **flowers**, and **symbols** within the image. Close your eyes and see the details in your mind, **repeating** the clockwise **motion**. **Continue** this process for the **second** five minutes or until the image is firmly **established** in your mind. In the last five minutes, sit **quietly**, waiting for any **message** that the image **might** have for **you**.

```
F O L V S X S A Q P Z M T Q A W N N L M
U H E X D C Z X B V D K H S A R T L B Y
Z B K W U M K J U N K X T M U A Z X S S
L V X C W P Z Z A P B P V T F D Z F R F
T Z I V O N M Q D O R X E S E G A M I H
C S O R L R Q O S E G R R T R Y A V Y R
U P W C L A Y R P A S M A I A F E F W F
M E S S A G E E R C N I G E B L I B N H
J L I Y N W A E B U L E G E Y E S U F Q
B S I U O T N L I N V J F N W N M C L M
V E R L I Z U T U I R O P S S E R P M I
M I F N T A E S T A B L I S H E D Z H G
G I G N N H U C L O C K W I S E C M H H
L R N T E O U O V E R A L L L R F O K T
E E P U T R I N Y L M N L O O P K N N M
C C O B T O B T M J R K H J B O C O O D
Q Q J S A E Z I I Y O W E B M U U T E Q
U W N I W F S N N S F X S Q Y Y I I T L
Q O R W K T V U D I O S D E S O L C G V
C L D J Y L T E I U Q P B W N B D E U V
```

Solution on page 175

USE INTENTION TO DISCOVER YOUR LIFE'S PURPOSE

You may feel **perfectly** in **step** with your life's plan and in **tune** with its **purpose**. But if not, use this twelve-step **heart chakra** meditation. Put forth an **intention** to gain **direction** if you **desire** to be **guided** toward your best life now.

1. **Kneel** on your **yoga** mat, sitting on your **heels** (knees together, heels **touching**).

2. Lean **forward**, allowing your **forehead** to come down to **rest** on the mat.

3. Place your **hands**, palms up, **beside** your feet. **Relax** your toes. (This is called the Child's Pose.)

4. **Inhale** slowly and **breathe** out through your nose.

5. **Surrender** all the **tension** in your **shoulders** and body into the **earth** as your thoughts **follow** the **stream** of breath in for five to ten **cycles**.

6. **Rise** back to the sitting **position**, making sure **toes** are relaxed, arms are at your back, and **fingers** are laced **together** before you **stretch**.

7. Keeping your **spine** straight and **facing** up, stretch **backward** to **open** your **chest** and heart chakra.

8. Inhale and feel **blessings** for **knowledge** and all you **need** in your life coming to you.

9. **Exhale** and feel the **release** of that which you don't need in your life **floating** away. Repeat the inhale/**accept** and exhale/release for five to ten cycles.

10. Move out of that pose to rest in a cross-legged **asana**, palms open on your **thighs**. Feel your heart **energy** enlivened; **mentally** state your **desire** to have your best life now—to know your **purpose** and whether to stay the **course** or change direction.

11. Rest in heart-centered **awareness**.

12. Note feelings of **peace** versus uneasiness (yes/no **responses** from your **intuition**).

```
G L E L J B F A S P I N E E N U T M Y F
N E T Z N J C X L R B Y S I P E A C E L
G E S R U O C A E E R I S E D E H G X Z
B N E T E D I S E B R A W A R E N E S S
A K F D R K T T H E G N I T A O L F G I
T O E S R E G N I F G Y S R W P O Q N D
C S H G I H T O K S G D T D R E C C I F
I W Q K A E R C R I O C E L O N H R S O
B P U R P O S E H T H P T L F J E I S L
I A G O Y P D S S A P N W N W C S Z E L
V W C X C L E U K P H E O O T O T I L O
R Z N K U L S R E N O I T I U T N I B W
H E D O W O A R F G C N O S T G I K K J
G E H T H A F E O E Y N S N E N E R G Y
U S N T A U R N R I C R R E A I E V H F
I A C C E P T D E N L T E T S H A T A A
D E L T R G P E H H E X L A A C R N N C
E L A H X E O R E A S D A Y N U T I D I
D E D O M E N T A L L Y X W A O H V S N
E R V H R F Z W D E L B R E A T H E F G
```

Solution on page 176

DAYDREAM FOR TWENTY MINUTES EVERY MORNING

Daydreaming can **stimulate** your mind in **creative** ways, **reduce** stress, **elevate** your **mood**, organize your **thinking**, stimulate **ideas** for **solutions** to problems, and help you **gain** new **perspectives** on troubling **issues**. Assuming that you are not using **daydreams** to **escape** from being fully **engaged** in your life or **retreating** from your **responsibilities**, then a **regular** period of daydreaming is not only **healthy**, but **helpful** in solving problems and **fostering** creativity. Set a **timer**. Let your **thoughts** take flight to a **Greek** island, a **trekking** path high in the **Himalayas**, a **manicured** estate in **England**, a **beach** in **Barbados**, or somewhere else; **indulge** yourself. Let your thoughts take **flight**.

```
N D U Z J Q G Q U F Z E K L U F P L E H
S F P E F H N S N O I T U L O S W N S B
J E H B O M E B M N M K S T V N G A I N
X O I O S B A A W A U F I X M L X J U G
C Y H T T H S J L B E M S T A G R S B Y
K V G N I T A E R T E R R N K X B H G G
G E E Q M L F T U R H E D X R J I N S A
P W P F U H I N P S K Y P Y S M I I I E
H M I E L O X B B K S E P B A R N U L N
Z Z R S A I A B I A R I U L E D G E Q G
S X E M T B G N Q S E O A T U M V U X A
E B D D E H G H P Z N Y S L L A G T N G
I A U E O A G E T C A O G E T N H B D E
A R C X V V C U V S F E P E S I H D X D
I B E U R T S O O I L B C S N C S K G B
J A D G I F Y E I H T T H K E U A R T Q
D D S V U K H L Q W T A I I W R E P Z L
M O E B P L W L W G Z N E C W E D I E C
O S O W G C A W K K G W A R K D I P C P
Q S C M Z A I R A Y D B E A C H Z L Y X
```

Solution on page 176

HOW MANTRAS WORK

In the **Middle East**, you will **hear** the call to **prayer** five **times** a day. In **Europe**, the **church** bells sound **daily**. At **Japanese** shrines, wind **chimes** produce **soothing** sounds. In these **cultures**, sounds both **awaken** the **listener** and prepare for **quieter** moments, reminding everyone that **peaceful** times are **approaching**.

When entering into a **meditation**, we must first empty **ourselves** of thought. **Reciting** mantras and **toning** sounds **facilitates** this process. **Repetitive** auditory **signals**, especially if they are **produced** in a **calming**, consistent manner, **relax** thought. Then, **launching** into **stillness** requires less **effort**. It's **important** to **remember** that the **science** of **mantra** is a tool of meditation, but it is not meditation. Only when the **mind** is still is one in a **state** of meditation.

```
V Q W F H M D T B F Y P H Z I W S D Q D
V V V F D N T L R X G C Y P R E U V B V
X O B V C N N L J P R D N I M C D L H A
A T S Q A T I L A U N C H I N G Y D T A
G Z U I F Q C U H H D O T T Q Y K F C A
S Y R H D M B C T G D A I L Y C T H C I
N D C R B S L A N G I S X T E S I D R K
Q R T Q H E Q H A W E B K Y A M N E S J
T W L S G N I H T O O S I E E T T C E B
R E B M E M E R R W L K E S S E I U V G
O U C Z V T J W O F I L E N I U E D L N
F R L N X M A F P G D R P U A V N O E I
F O I U G A M T M D U A Q X I P R R S M
E P S S E N L L I T S C W T V E A P R L
T E T S E T X M L L F I I A L C R J U A
M O E M T R B U Y H I T W A K N P X O C
J I N O S A C G E J E C X G R E Y A R P
S W E I Z G T A P P R O A C H I N G G Y
E Q R I N U R E E A N L U F E C A E P Z
C I H O P G D R E C I T I N G S T W U Q
```

Solution on page 176

DON'T LET THIS MOMENT PASS YOU BY

How **often** are you **barely** able to **concentrate** on what you're **doing** because of all the to-dos in your **life**, and all the thoughts **weighing** on your mind? You now have a good **reason** to start **slowing** down, taking a **pause** throughout your day, and **giving** yourself "me" time. The **good** reason is your overall well-being. If you **continue** to go, go, go, whether **physically**, mentally, or both, then it's **likely** that you don't take **time** to be in the **moment** as often as your body **needs**. When you're going on **autopilot** with so much **thinking**, doing, and **moving**, your body gets out of **balance**. You might **notice** this in a **variety** of ways: weight loss or **gain**, mental or **emotional** fatigue, depression, lack of **motivation**, feeling overwhelmed, getting **easily** irritated, losing your **keys**, or losing **sleep**. All of these are **signs** that your body isn't **functioning** in the way it works best, and **according** to **chakra** theory, your chakras will be out of balance. The first step in **helping** your body back to **health** and balancing the chakras is learning to drop into the **present** moment, to stop thinking, doing, and **going**. **Allow** yourself to be.

```
N Q L S N Z P A M S G N I O G H J C V C
V E E S T E D W N F F E Q R Q I P T K G
B X S V H J E K Y T J B Q Y A R V N N P
N O U P A I G D O G J H E A L T H I K M
W O A O G R N L S L E E P A J E K F N K
R O P H Y S I C A L L Y I I E N R X A G
P O I O Z P N E P Y E M O T I O N A L N
Q N G C O C O N T I N U E H S O Z M B O
G O S T O B I M B Y C A T M I G D S A T
N S U P I N T G X I Q H K T O F T E N I
W A V S K N C R R U G B A L A N C E N C
Y E D Q E O N E K G N V A K H Z S K Q E
C R O M Y P U S N G I S N O R E Y U G I
L V O W S G F I A T D G M R R A L N O E
X M G A B A W C O W R M I P G N I O D T
T F W T G O Z M G B O A A U G P S G I P
Y F U N L U H V A V C L T Z L S A M S A
H X R S W I J T I Y C H L E Y L E K I L
T C Q X Q L F N N E A I H A N V N U N Z
S T I C Z T G E P X Y K V I T O J Z E K
```

Solution on page 177

KEEP AN OPEN HEART BY WISHING OTHERS WELL

As you are **practicing** enjoying the **moment** now and also manifesting things for the **future**, keep an open **heart**. This is not as **easy** as it **sounds**. The heart is very **perceptive**, and as such it will **close** down to **protect** itself. If you are **expending** too much attention **outward** or if you are being **overloaded** with too much needy **attention**, the heart will become **blocked**. You can **open** your heart when it will serve you by **focusing** on your heart **chakra**.

Send **loving** thoughts from your heart chakra to your **friends** and **loved** ones to help **keep** your heart open. You can also hold a **specific** person in your mind's eye, and send them a powerful wish: "May you be **happy**. May you be **healthy**. May you know **peace**." When you are **truly** able to wish **everyone** peace and happiness, **even** those with whom you feel conflict, you will **know** your heart is open. When you **balance** your heart chakra, you are **connected** to the feeling of **oneness** of all that is. That's the **space** to be in as you **manifest** your own **desires**.

```
H F F Y M Q D W S M L G S W N T I T U K
S Y M H K I D J I D M V Z G O H Y V C P
Q A S V D R H L X X N T Y H T N Q K G T
Z X V G X G K W Z R S C B L O C K E D Y
D K G G M N U T P E R C E P T I V E R Z
Z E B G H I D C H A K R A B A G D S A V
J L C S E V K E G N I C I T C A R P W W
L P T L R O A G S P Z E H I O T H Z T F
N G N Y U L E V N I E S O L C T E H U A
R O T U T U C H J I R V R D U E C L O M
V H P H U P A E Y G D E T C E N N O C N
O A Y E F T P V N Y V N S H U T A V O D
K A T G N I S U C O F M E F K I L E Z U
P E C I F I C E P S Y R O P Y O A D S O
D Q E D Y S A E F U O R Z M X N B S I X
H L T P U M A T G I Y X E M E E E N T Z
Z N O Q T C F R I E N D S V W N V B A H
J W R N E R X U F T R A E H E Q T E B K
H A P P Y V E L Y L U O M N H X F Z N O
O L U K G Z F Y K M U S O U N D S Z O B
```

Solution on page 177

THE POWER OF INFINITE POSSIBILITY

Stories abound of **ancient** yogis who had the **power** to **create** or **bestow** health, **wealth**, happiness, and **spiritual** powers—even **enlightenment**. It is possible for you to claim that power as **well** when you set forth the **intention** to have success, **abundance** without limit, excellent **health**, dynamic willpower, and wisdom. **Remember** that you are the **architect** of your life, cocreating with the **Divine** Power that has created the **Universe** and everything that **moves** in it. **Properly** aligned with that **Higher** Power's **dynamic** force and **wisdom**, you tap into the **realm** of **possibility** and potentiality. You attract **synchronicity** into your life along with those **blessings** of health, wealth, **happiness**, and spiritual powers that you may **seek**.

1. **Close** your eyes.

2. **Breathe** in a **natural**, easy rhythm as you **relax** into a **cocoon** of **peace**.

3. Think of Divine Will as **limitless** energy (**capable** of creating **solar** systems or changing **destiny**, for example) guided by wisdom.

4. **Feel** your will **attuning** to Divine Will.

5. Know that the abundance from the **storehouse** of the Universe can flow **freely** to you when you **unite** your will with the Higher Power.

6. **Before** exerting your will, **align** it with that Higher Power so that you might tap into the highest source of **confidence** and abundance for **success**.

```
K R D M Q M Y J A B U N D A N C E U U M
J M H K O M Y T I C I N O R H C N Y S G
I D Z T D V Z C R W V B C T V I L L E W
O I Y Y L R E P O R P L C D V S I G A E
C V Y N E A E S O Z O E L E S A G U Z F
R L H W A H E K K S T S R E L G H B R H
N F O S T M G H E I S S N I O R T E F I
O P W A T E I P H O E I G Y A D E B C G
E I E E U O L C V E P N B L O L N E O S
B R A T N Z R B K P Q G O I Y C M F C B
B C L A I A P E A C E S N Y L A E O O T
D P T E N W O H H P T L O M I I N R O W
F Y H R G F Q I L O A A I S Z F T E N L
G C N C E S L L R A U C T M I W L Y M S
C V C I D M V I D O R S N D I O G O L U
A J W O T N E I C N A U E L D T D R A C
K L Z U D S V M Q R N N T O E S L A E C
B U A E G I E S B S C R N A I E Q E R E
V E T I N U Z D A E U F I W N B F C S S
X A L E R H I G H E R L A U T I R I P S
```

Solution on page 177

USE A GRATITUDE REMINDER

If you're like most **people**, you **might** be totally **committed** to the **idea** of doing **something** but end up scolding **yourself** at the end of the day **because** you forgot to do it! Our **lives** are so **packed** with **activities** and **appointments** that it's totally **understandable** when something falls through the **cracks**.

To make sure **practicing** gratitude doesn't fall through the cracks, here's a **handy** trick: Set a gratitude **reminder** on your **phone**. You can set it for whatever **time** works for you, whether that's **first** thing in the **morning**, at lunchtime, right after you get **home**, or just before **bed**. When the reminder **pops** up on your phone, take just **five** minutes—or even two **minutes**, if you're really low on time—to **think** about what you are **grateful** for today. It could be something **small**, like the **barista** getting your **coffee** just right this morning, or something **bigger**, like the job that allows you to pay your **bills**.

Setting a reminder will make you **much** more **likely** to find the time to be grateful. **Just** make sure you don't dismiss the reminder before you actually **engage** in your **gratitude** practice—that's a good way to **forget**.

```
S Z U D C F B A N K M U D Y C Y F P L T
J D Q B J I V A G N I N R O M Y M Z A O
Y K G T E C L P C A E D I J H D I F L J
Y Z G N I T T E S O M E T H I N G U U S
P D R G N I C I T C A R P U P A H S P N
S F V U V A E T R D R S D S H H T O C M
B E B B B I S T N E M T N I O P P A K X
D I T B Q R Q J D T D A P L N S R C G E
T D V U I Z U U P T C N X L E F I T V O
E U J F N H T R W I U D I A H L Q I F I
R S S N Y I R Z R M Q A L M C E F V O K
T K U Z T L M G S M Y B J S E S H I R C
L S E A O R E P G O S L F C M R S T G R
Y K R K C D U K E C H E U V C U C I E A
D G V Y R E G G I B C L V F G O F E T C
J T H I N K B S L L U P K I E Y F S N K
Z Y G E C C T I M E M O H X L T I F N S
F Y M A Q A X X L Y J E P O R R A D E B
C E O Z G P M R F L K P O Y A P Y R L E
D K F X E Y T H T U S Q T B E N G A G E
```

Solution on page 178

HAVE A GLASS OF WINE AT THE END OF A DIFFICULT DAY

Unwind with a **glass** of your favorite **wine** at the end of an exhausting **day**. **According** to a number of **research** findings, wine is **good** for you if you **drink** it in **moderation** and as part of a **healthy** diet. Wine has **nonalcoholic** phytochemicals (**flavonoids** and **resveratrol**) that can prevent free **radical** molecules from damaging your body's **cells**. **Studies** show that wine reduces the **risk** of getting **certain** cancers and also **heart** disease, as well as slowing the **progression** of Alzheimer's and Parkinson's disease. For **women**, one five-**ounce** glass a day is good, but the health **benefits** are forfeited if you drink **more**.

```
E D L Q X F X O M T K B C C L H D D M K
R S T Q G E D F U O G S P Z R U D O O F
D J U W G C V Z L Q R T R A E H I R D W
V H O N O N O I T A R E D O M P E Y D V
K H G N O M H M X M V I N G U N Y H T Q
C J C O D N E K N U C O M P D E K X C O
L D R K R B A N R A Z C N R G D J F G G
Q L E B H S L L L X J L I O I M H F L S
R T X Y L D T V C R L N W G I S Z W A S
J X M R K O H S L O K X N R L D K F S G
M C J U C E Y M R E H G I E Y J S L S P
G O I S E P P T N V Q O V S V P A L P G
K C E H Y M A S W I N E L S S C L I L Q
W B O Y O R W X G P A Y M I C E J B S X
U B E N E F I T S G C T Q O C S N J H Q
B H J V G H C R A E S E R N E O F C G D
V A S W I I I F H B C P D S E I D U T S C
V E S Y A N F Q L U I F A F C W T N R K
R I T X U U N W I N D T W Y Y L O B C D
Y T R H H T L X G L S W P Q K G E Z X E
```

Solution on page 178

VOLUNTEER AT AN ANIMAL SHELTER

Volunteer your free **time** at your local **animal** shelter. You **will** be a volunteer **parent** to a **lonely**, even **possibly** abandoned or abused, animal. You may be **asked** to **help** in **various** ways, including **transporting** animals to their **veterinarian** appointments, **participating** in **community** activities that **foster** animal **adoptions**, educating the **public** about the **need** for **humane** treatment of animals, **cleaning** out animal cages, and **reuniting** lost pets with their **owners**, to **name** a few. For animal **lovers**, such **work** can not only be **satisfying**; it can give **meaning** and **purpose** to their lives. And those are **vital** elements of **life** satisfaction and **happiness**.

```
Y I E L T A H K L A M I N A J A X M L P
L S U P H Z V L R D Y L I F E D G E C G
O I R E E T N U L O V F S S O N P K I I
N O Y C I B H Y T P W S P U I J A H L H
S A I M L J F S Z T L V A T V Y K M B Z
G L F D X N A W P I H A R E G A M O U M
A A K T A S R E V O L O T N R X K E P H
S Y L V K G Y A N N P E I I W V D S C Q
G H Y E T M F T I S R Y C N V P E O L F
T S D F Q D L L N I F H I X A E M P E F
Z F P O V G X A N S G B P A V M U R A M
V Y N T U A R A I S M Q A O U I E U N C
S G H Y Z T R T B G S I T N S T O P I S
I O Y L A I A I U N T E I N K S A T N E
D M W E A S G W O Z N T N J E Z I U G G
R E U N I T I N G U Y T G I K R L B X N
H K L O E G I R E T S O F L P P A Q L D
F R A L I R X C D U X K Y J O P L P E Y
B I Y R I S S W D O K O G N I N A E M H
R J K G H W M U H H C Q M I N I N I N H H Q
```

Solution on page 178

THE SERENE MIND ENGENDERS JOY

The **inwardly** turned **mind** that is not **asleep**, not thinking, and yet alert produces **physiological** changes in the body. Slower **breathing** drives down **blood** pressure and **heart** rate. As your **oxygen** consumption goes **down**, your mind—in a state of **relaxed** awareness—begins to behold itself and **experience** joy. This is the **foundation** for the **meditation** and **contemplation** practiced by **saints** and **sages** over time throughout the world. This meditation brings a **joyful** peace. As the **Buddha** notes, "Joy follows a pure **thought** like a **shadow** that never **leaves**."

1. With eyes **closed**, direct your **attention** to the **space** between your **brows**. This will be your **focal** point for this meditation. **Gently** gaze into that space without **straining**.

2. As thoughts or **emotions** arise to threaten your **peace**, don't try to **reason**, deny, or argue them away. That **would** be **conflicting** and counterproductive, derailing your meditation. Don't be **hard** on yourself but rather **practice** patience and **loving-kindness**. Maintain a detached **awareness** of what **arises** during meditation.

3. In Buddhism, **inner** peace isn't a **static** condition. It is a **dynamic** state **brimming** with **insight**, perception, **knowledge**, and compassion.

4. **Hold** on to the awareness of that inner peace. Carry that joyful **serenity** unhindered into your day.

```
H M S E G A S M D M H F H K O H G S V R
D X T U Y J N M I N N E R Q P E E L S A
V S A I N T S S E N E R A W A L S N I J
O R T F N G A I H Z D X O R C L O S E D
B R I M M I N G J F R S P Y T I D L O H
O L C N A N O I T A L P M E T N O C P I
W N O X W Q O V T X E A R O R V C M E R
P O O O Q A P I X C M C M A I I W T A E
M S D I D Z R H T A I E H N C T E J C L
Q A W A T S F D Y A Z L G E L T O N E A
A E W S H A U N L S D K F I I Y I A C X
R R B Y E S T O G Y I N Q N F O V C H E
I T U O P R W I X N A O U U O E Y R E D
S H D O W N E T D Y I K L O S C O G P L
E G D E L W O N K E G H Q O F O C A L U
S I H A R D E E I C M E T H G U O H T O
V S A F A S B T N T D Y N A M I C R V W
P N A P S D U T I C Y L T N E G C R D Q
P I G N I N I A R T S A S W O R B A T W
R S V W B G U B H G J M K N Y E B B L J
```

Solution on page 179

A CANDLE MEDITATION

Candles are a **popular** way to **scent** living **space** and add **festivity** to a gathering. You can find just about any size, **shape**, color, or **fragrance** to complement your décor. For **meditation** practice, candles can also **provide** an **atmosphere** that supports your **intentions**. In addition, they offer their own little **rituals** that **reflect** your **goals**.

Choose a candle **color** that reflects your intentions. Select a scent that **embodies** your goals. **Devote** a full **session** to the candle meditation. Dim the lights but avoid a completely **dark** room. **Begin** by **assembling** a candle, matches or **lighter**, candleholder, and **snuffer**. Use a separate **table** or **stand** for the candle. **Allow** yourself five minutes to **attain** even **breathing** and physical **composure**. As you are doing this, **close** your eyes and **think** of your mind as a candle, awaiting **illumination**.

Strike the **match** or lighter with a flourish. Keep your eyes on the **flame** as you light the candle. **Gaze** at the flame and think of it as the **spirit** of illumination that is lighting your **mind**. Give **yourself** twenty-five minutes to gaze. When you put out the candle, do so **deliberately**. Understand that the spirit of illumination can **enter** your life whenever you give it **attention** by lighting the candle.

```
D P E N S T S N G G E M A L F G J T S I
Y C F F P J Q G P O B S I L A R W P G A
Z I R E A O D H H W S E E N D C R O Z X
E D A S C Y P Z J R E S G E D D I G H A
A H G T E T I U X H R Z L U N N N S B Y
B C R I T N I L L U M I N A T I O N D R
H Z A V W E N F O A B R T E L A I M E E
N R N I N C N Y V E R S N B F T T N V F
T Z C T D S Z T R F P T M H C T A M O F
A G E Y C T A A I E I E J R Y A T E T U
B R O C P J T F M O S F P R O V I D E N
L Q I Y L E M B N S N G K C A N D L E S
E I U Z L O O S A S G N I H T A E R B L
E F G Y V D S W R F E R U S O P M O C A
R P Q H I X P E C E E S O O H C O P O U
Y E B E T E H A K K Q S S P I R I T L T
M B S P G E E I L E B E G I N M I G O I
K J O A X H R E F L E C T G O A L S R R
H L Z H W T E N Z D O E T H I N K R A D
Q E S S S E G M V N H W B J D E K A X X
```

Solution on page 179

RELINQUISH WORRY TO A HIGHER POWER

Paramahansa **Yogananda** asserted, "When you have **peace** in every **movement** of your body…thinking…willpower…**love**, and peace and God in your **ambitions**, remember—you have **connected** God with your life." Feeling protected and at peace is **easy** when you **accept** that you are not in control and turn over all your **concern** to a Higher **Power**. The best **balm** for a burdened mind is to stop fretting and **settle** down. Worry **gives** rise to a **deeper** delusion within you. **Quiet** your **heart** and **still** your **mind**. Use the following **simple** breathing **technique** to re-establish **equilibrium** in your consciousness before **making** your positive **affirmation** for **protection** and peace.

1. **Inhale** to the count of six.

2. **Hold** for a count of six.

3. **Exhale** to the count of **twelve**.

4. Hold the **breath** for a count of six.

5. **Repeat** these steps ten or more times and then affirm: "I am protected by the **Divine**, whose **spirit** is **before** me, **behind** me, **beneath** me, **above** me, to the **left** of me and the **right**. I have **nothing** to fear within or **without**. All is as it **should** be, according to Divine Will. I am at peace."

```
D E G P G U E W P G H W J Z B M E Z M D
R Q D O E I J N N Q T A E P E R X F I R
W J E I F Y V D T W Y T Z U F T B V M Z
R J K H X Y Y E I W D T N U O C I A S P
T D C Y T F A T S P O W E R R N G M P U
J P P O G S H C M H Z A C C E P T Q T N
U W R G Y O Y E L A H N I F T C T F V A
V N W K U P L N A D R S Y P X W N U K A
V K S T M A R N B D C S E T T L E O U B
X O P N H M Y O G A N A N D A M M L C O
Z L H X O D U C T E C H N I Q U E V V V
Z N E L A I E I L E F T B V N V V W A E
G K S E L A T E R E C A E P O L O J W S
M N P A L I O I P B B T U L T R M U X I
C H I D H P T T B E I I I S H O U L D M
V F R K T R M S H M R L K O I T W R M G
B I I X A F F I R M A T I O N F S I J O
A W T E E M N R S I A I F U G N N G W U
S M H J R D L O H K T E I U Q D G H P C
Y X M A B H F W Q N T E B E N E A T H T
```

Solution on page 179

COUNT YOUR LOOSE CHANGE AND DONATE IT

For a **quick** dose of **happiness**, gather up that **loose** change lying around the **house** and give it to a good **cause**. By some **estimates**, the average **American** household has as **much** as $90 lying under the **sofa** cushions, in **dresser** drawers, and even in **laundry** rooms where a lot of it comes out in the **wash**. There are **myriad** ways to **donate** your loose **change**—drop the **coins** into **charity** boxes in **grocery** store **checkout** lines, give it to your **church** or **temple**, or simply convert it to **currency** and donate it to a **favorite** charitable **organization**. Happiness **researchers** say that when you **perform** a **selfless** act of **generosity** for someone else, it **increases** your happiness.

T D C Q Z W X P D U W D A U Y Q G X Q B
H S A W S S Y C Q J T I S G V F H M I A
N R E S S E R D S I K Z C I C P H A S K
I S R L Z X Y E Y A N M X Z H M H M I R
S W M A F O S J C H E C K O U T U G G U
Q C D U Z L T Y R E C O R G S O R C C C
F E H L S R E H C R A E S E R U S A H J
U U K U Y T I S O R E N E G A S O A A S
H P Y A R R H E S T I M A T E S N M R X
Z K Y Y D C H J Q O W N E N N G E A I C
Y E T X N W H C U O I M I I E R F S T S
C P J C U G V D M Z P P O C I M E S Y P
J W E H A N Z I A L P C Y C N E R R U C
C U B R L Q M T E A X F A V O R I T E K
T D J U F D I O H D O N A T E Y D S C X
D R A Q R O W O A C A U S E Q S O I T Z
W D D M N W R B T U J I L D Z O U M G M
V D N V H J E M U L A F R C L Q V O I G
M U S H Q Q G D J M Q F R Y S S L T H Q
Q K O J F G C S O T H S I G M C S L H P

Solution on page 180

A MINDFUL EXERCISE

An **exercise** in **mindfulness** meditation usually **starts** by focusing on the **physical** body and then **moving** to the mind. Start by using a **technique** of "**scanning**" or "**sweeping**" the body from **bottom** to **top**. Start with the **feet**; move up in **sequence** to the **calves**, thighs, **torso**, arms, neck, and **head**.

Move your **focus** slowly. With eyes closed, **train** your **attention** on each **section** of your body. Note the sensations of **heat** and **cold**, the air on your **skin**, the texture of the **muscles**, any stiffness, any pulsing **sensations**. Give yourself ten **minutes** for this.

When you have **finished** with your head, move your attention to **breathing**. Note its **evenness** and **rhythm**. Give yourself **five** minutes for this. Now **relax** your attention and **observe** your **thoughts**. If thinking **interferes** with observing, go **back** to scanning your **body**.

```
M P W G M P G L D X X T Y O Z L U Y B V
P K L U U H N L E W N C C V M N D N R W
L S W A S K C A B R O G H E P I V E N F
E K G G C I N M R J I B N E V A I O I T
J I W W L I X H E H T H T I A R I V O S
M G R F E X S T A N C F A C P T E R L P
B R Z I S N N Y T K E V E N N E S S T E
D Y E N A I G H H T S W S E E O E E B I
E R M I K H T R I P B O T T O M E W G O
O B U S F N S S N O I T A S N E S N S E
U I T H Z I E S G D A N T C I S I W W K
E Z U E L K Q I T L R A Q U E N C G D T
G C P D C S U H G H R E I N N D R N T W
E V M O N H E V S T G D L A Y M E D S R
W G L Y I A N U S E H U C A G I X X X C
L D T S D I C I B I F S O P X N E Z A S
M S F M R O E R Q D R J F H O U I L G X
Z L W G F F B D N U H E P M T T V V X H
W O Y C F K F I N T E R F E R E S C O C
B S H T G E M X P T K S Q H S S H E O M
```

Solution on page 180

KEEP YOUR PROMISES
TO OTHERS

One way to spread **happiness** is to keep your **promises**. Just as you see **someone** who is **faithful** to her word as trustworthy, so your **friends**, family, and business **colleagues** will also **trust** you when you **hold** to the truth. In this age of **spin**, when **facts** get altered in ways to **deliberately** mislead **people** and to further **ideological** agendas, let your truth be **absolute**.

It isn't **always** easy to **align** your **feelings**, thoughts, **beliefs**, and spoken words so that no one **questions** your truthfulness or **integrity**. **Gandhi** used truth as his **nonviolent** weapon against **adversaries**. No one **questioned** his truthfulness or whether he could **keep** his promises to others. **Imagine** the happiness of **millions** of **Indians** when his Quit India **movement** secured their **freedom** from the **British**.

```
W M S K G Q G M I A K S H U A I A V I Q
Y X O G J T O D P A S I W R K T S M S V
X H T V A D A E O L A B S O L U T E R S
U R N L E N R A S I Z S E S I M O R P U
R H N E M M D B N G E U L V U J T Q I Z
E X R F J Y E H O N X F A I T H F U L M
I F J I M L Z N I S J O C P Z G Y D W O
T B I K Y E X P T T E F I R E Q L M I W
B H N M O T P R S P N M G N M O W N V T
G D T I W A W V E D H E O N H B P G E F
C J E T H R S E U G A E L L O C V L T M
O Q G N F E K E Q K M W O O I L W X E D
Q N R A O B N Y V O V D E S I F S H U S
H L I S E I R A S R E V D A F V G I N T
H S T P G L T I T L N N I I N E N O D C
S T Y A S E W S T P E E K K H D I O H A
Q W M A J D U E E I P B L S I L L L N F
Z I L S W R D B R U S I H A L S E P E Y
T F T T T L U F E N Q H N I S O E N N B
V T X M X Y A S K M N S M B T X F W M S
```

Solution on page 180

EVERYDAY MOVING MEDITATIONS

You may **think** that **meditation** in some **places** and **environments** is difficult, if not impossible. For **instance**, you may **find** yourself **waiting** in line, stuck in **traffic**, or stuffed in a **crowded** doctor's waiting **room**. With **nothing** to do but wait, **restlessness** can easily set in. And there's nothing more irritating than waiting around with the **person** nearest you **fidgeting** nervously while **another** is **rattling** coins or **keys** in his pocket. Your **inner** voice may be crying, "Get me out of here!"

Instead, **focus** on a **peaceful** scene **around** you. It may be **depicted** in a **painting** on the wall or **outside** through a **window**. A **sleeping** baby in someone's **arms**, a **lovely** tree in full **bloom**, or a **patient**, elderly person waiting **nearby** can provide the **visual** support that says to you, "**Everything** is moving in the right **rhythm**, and so am I." The **daily** grind asks much of the inner **resources**, and meditation can **support** you **along** the way.

```
Z H H H X S S S U P P O R T Y L I Y F G
L R B X W E T E U U R S E C A L P C W E
Q W E G K U N C T C T S D C R G I G K V
E P T N L N E R U P O Y W E I O G A T Q
G D I W N O M U P S H F S U P F W T D P
X H O J W I N O G N I T E G D I F D Q M
T K U G O T O S C Y L A W V C I C A E R
Y G G M R A R E V E R Y T H I N G T R D
R G J J Z T I R S M A S P B V S S P E T
O Y M X K I V S S L T P A I N T I N G D
O H H B E D N A N O T H E R P A J Y L M
M W B Z Y E E B O G L A R O U N D U H Y
I O U J S M O I T G I B W G I C F T A Y
Y N O S R E P X H N N B F K B E Y N N L
P T K L V E B T I I G I Y Z C H W E U E
W H S C B X C T N T V B P A R O X I Y V
J X X W D H W F G I R C E E D I S T U O
T S L U W V I S U A L P D N E R Q A P L
N B Z Q T N A J E W A P I I J O L G P S J
N H S X D J G N O L A W I H R E S N W Y
```

Solution on page 181

Being in the body can be a **pleasurable** experience. All of your **senses** have the **capability** to **bring** pleasure into your **life**: Your eyes see the **colors** of a **sunset** and your sense of **touch** feels a soft **breeze** on your body. All it takes is a **moment** to **experience** the **beauty** of life **around** you and just "be." In **addition** to **appreciating** the senses, taking care of **your** body can be **enjoyable**. The body wants to **move**, wants to be **nourished**, and wants to be **healthy**. Your life **force** wants to flow **freely** through you. If you haven't **taken** care of yourself for a while, at first it **might** seem **difficult** to start new **habits**. Then, in just a **little** bit of **time** you will start to **notice** a **difference**; you will feel the **urge** to keep taking **good** care because it will feel good. **Taking** care of yourself also can be **fun**: It's about finding the **right** activities for you and bringing an open-minded, positive **outlook** to the **process**. Soon you will feel a difference and the **desire** to **keep** up with your new habits.

```
F Y Q P U C V M M Q A T N S E H G R M U
K B K G A H F D P X P L G S Z Y I S O M
A Q G Q N D A S E S N E S P J H Q G C T
O M R S W I D B V H K O O L T U O R M J
E P S P E F E I I Y S F R E E L Y I Z L
E D C G L G G B T T D I O A D T A K E N
B O V C N F R U J I S H R S L P O P C Y
N O T I C E I U F L O X Z U P W R U M K
R G R S E S R F A I K N S R O L O C C L
C B H Z Y B I E X B F E E A W N Z D Y H
K W E R O C G A X A R C Q B W C E E N I
C D A A U H H C D P I N Q L E P N S R V
W C L L R U T U O A E E K E C E J I J X
P T T E S N U S T C V R S S E C O R P P
E I H E L T T I L O L E I L F R Y E Y S
H W Y G N T N E M I T F I E U O A Z J Q
M G X E I G N I K A T F W L N F B F K X
C W M N U M C C Y A E I D C M C L E Z B
P O X H D D A R O U N D Y T U A E B T R
M Z T I A B A P D Z Q B I B C P W C B G
```

Solution on page 181

MINDFULNESS VERSUS CONCENTRATION

Mindfulness does not **mean** that you are completely **focused** on washing the **dishes** and your **concentration** is so **complete** that all else **recedes** into the **background** and all that is left is the **water** and the dishes. Mindfulness means to be **aware** of **everything**. Mindfulness is entering into the **moment** with an awareness of all that **surrounds** you. When we try to **unravel** a **knot** in a thin gold **chain**, we are concentrating. We are completely focused on the knot—we are not aware of our **fingers**, our **breath**, the **coolness** of the air, or the **shaft** of **sunlight** coming in the **nearby** open **window**.

Concentration and mindfulness are not the **same** thing, but they work together as a **team**. In **order** to have a meditation **practice** that is working, you must have the **power** of concentration and the **power** of mindfulness. Concentration **allows** you to focus on one thing. Mindfulness allows you to become aware of the focus, and to take **note** when it **strays**. Concentration **without** mindfulness is not a **successful** meditation practice. Mindfulness allows you to **notice** that your **attention**—your concentration—is **slipping**. Mindfulness is the part of you that notes, "The **door** is opening, the **bird** is singing," while you continue to concentrate on one **point**, whether that be a **task**, your breath, or your **koan**.

When we are mindful, we are concentrating. But when we are concentrating, we are not **always** mindful. We can unravel the knot in a **gold** chain in a mindful **state**. But it is much **more common** for most of us to concentrate without mindfulness. We **shut** down the parts of us that allow us to be mindful. We shut out the **world**.

```
U X D R E R O M K T H A S R H V I C T N
P X I I T E E A N W P K O A N C Q O X X
T B D E E J T E T C O O J T M V T H I F
U M K B L C M T N M D U W A T E R W X O
S I A T P O K I I S M N T E B N S I W H
L Y S P M R A R O L O R H V R O Z X M W
S X A U O H A V P I E A W E D I S H E S
V C Z W C L O C T P J V V R E T O N A C
S C O X L C T N T P D E J Y E A J R N S
A P X O M A E S C I J L B T B R E A T H
I R W X L T U S I N C J T H A T A A S A
K S A T T N T A S G S E D I N N T W T F
S Z W A L D E D O F M F I N G E R S A T
Y A V I A C N S D N U O R G K C A B T M
A T G T I U E S S E N L U F D N I M E L
R H U T O D R E D R O E J T U O H T I W
T H O R E A S B V L M P A F O C U S E D
S N R C G B G A B P M D L R O W D Z R L
K U E E Y T W I N D O W O Q B P K I W O
S R U P P N G B R D C C N I A Y B W R G
```

Solution on page 181

RELINQUISH THE NEED TO CONTROL

In this guided **meditation**, you will **discover** how much **easier** life can be when you set an **intention** and let go of the **need** to **control** how and when it comes. You will learn to **trust** that what is not **known** to you will become **clear** and what you've called **forth** in intention will be **manifested**, not **necessarily** in your time but in **accordance** with the **Divine Plan**.

1. Keep your **breathing** natural.

2. Still the **chatter** in your mind by linking a **numerical** count to each **inhalation** and the words "I am" to each **exhalation**, and **repeat** until you feel **relaxed** and your mind is **quiet**.

3. **Mentally** declare your intention—be **brief** and **specific**, stating your **desire** in a **positive** rather than a negative **declaration**. For **example**, avoid saying **something** like "I don't want to hear bad news about my **recent** job interview." Instead, say, "I **nailed** my job **interview** and **welcome** the manager's call to tell me, 'You're **hired**!'"

4. Trust that the **Universe** has **received** your intention declaration and is **responding** in **kind**.

5. Embrace **infinite** possibilities as you let go and **remember** the old adage "Each thing **comes** in its own **perfect** time."

```
T S E M O C R R J S B E L V N W O N K Z
A T B R W O R E X X A V H Y E M A J L Q
Q S I A E N R X P B R E A T H I N G D D
P X B H I T Z N F E X A M P L E M M I R
C O Z Y V R T D O H A M W E C E E G S S
D N I M R O Y A A I A T D U V C N N C Q
E U H J E L O L H N T I N T E N T I O N
Y H J D T D A X I C V A L H I A A H V U
W U G O N T I F N R W K R N O D L T E M
C E B W I I E T H N A F M A O R L E R E
D V L O O S K T A J D S I L L O Y M E R
A G N C T P R U L T L E S P F C O O C I
D A Q E O O O T A C I F E E Y C E S E C
F E D A F M S S T R J O I N C A T D N A
D A V E S R E V I N U R N I X E I S T L
D E S I R E W D O T B V C V H D N Z R T
P A O R E S P O N D I N G I R E I S A E
P E R F E C T R U S T V G D G R F P E I
K W T X S J E C I F I C E P S I N X L U
U D E X A L E R E M E M B E R H I D C Q
```

Solution on page 182

A COMMUTER'S MEDITATION

You may **experience** the whole **spectrum** of negative **emotions** if you have to **commute** to **work** every day. Frustration, **exasperation**, rage—all **result** in **stress**. By the time you get to work, you are probably **frazzled**, and the **coffee** isn't going to help. What can you do **while** driving that **will** get you to work in a **better** frame of **mind**?

Focus on **relaxing** your body. Pay **attention** to what your mind is **thinking** about. Be sure to **maintain** a **balance** of both body and mind. When you're commuting, **noises** are distracting but some can't be avoided. **Choose** uplifting **music** on the **radio** with **minimal** talk. **Eliminate** stressful news **updates** or **traffic** reports. Don't tap your **fingers**, feet, or **hands**, and avoid **honking** your car horn. **Visually** focus on **careful** driving. In the meantime, nurture yourself. **Stretch** and relax your hands, one at a **time**. To de-stress, **lift** your **shoulders** up to your ears, **release**. Practice **mantras**; use **tones** for **calming**.

```
Y A P W J M M U R T C E P S E S I O N R
H Q L X U Z Y E N A W Q T H I N K I N G
V B L S S D N A H H Y L L A U S I V U X
T F I L X V G Y S C A L M I N G C C A D
H C R I I R Z U T F T B V B C I O E W C
E D I P S W C M H H U E T E H S M A N A
U N J F R O B L M V G O R T O H M I B T
T I L M F Q O F F X N A O T O O U S L T
B M N Y X A M F X E I U F E S U T M J E
I A T J R I R Q S G K I A R E L E S X N
M N V H N K E T E Y N T S M G D W P V T
E T A I M H L R D G O I A C E E E S K I
B R M X B O E X E I H I X M M R I E J O
E A W O I D A R P O N S O A I S V T C N
L S L K N G S R K T G T D E L Z Z A R F
I E X A S P E R A T I O N W O E R D H G
H F Z A N S G I I O L C M U W E R P F M
W E J B U C N M N T E E E F F O C U B G
N U E L Q M E S T R E S S U Q T R J O V
X O T N I T Q S N M Y J L F Y N E K G T
```

Solution on page 182

Create a **bedtime** ritual for **yourself**. **Parents** are often **advised** to give their sleep-resistant **children** a **routine**, but the **technique** works for **grownups** too. Your routine **should** include a **series** of **steps** that are **conducive** to **relaxation**—for example, a **bath** or **shower**, then perhaps a few **minutes** of deep **breathing** or other relaxation technique; a cup of **herbal** tea; or a **good** book instead of the phone, **television,** or **computer**. Try not to get into the **habit** of falling **asleep** in **front** of the TV. **Once** in that habit, **falling** asleep **without** the TV will probably take **longer**, and you may not sleep as well. When your ritual is complete, **then** it's **lights** out.

```
W R S L E K M W D E M I T D E B G E R N
Z I E Q N J Z L U F B W J Q Q F C V E P
X W B D O C U Q A K L G C M O N U S R Q
L Q D Q G O I S E I R E S Y O D T S E H
K L V Q H N F R T N O I S I V E L E T M
V O O S H D I U M U Z X T R P Z C A U Q
Z O G C F U V H W X Z A C S U H B L P Q
J H E S M C F W T D X V Q P I O F Z M R
T T A R R I W E N A W J S L L R Y D O B
M U F B V C W L D E G D E T A E R C G
I J P Z I E W E O V D R N S L X B M K Q
U Y L V A T R S N L E O B I T V I R R K
E L N I Y O N Q G N S W D Z L N T H E N
F E S O U Y O O E P I N I C U L E P K H
O I M T R S G K R F V U P T Z O A R G U
C H I G H S N E L F D P E R H V E F A W
N N C O M G O O D P A S E J U O B I Y P
E F W X O N I P Y I N Z L W J F U Q H X
Y E E Q V H V L T O X S S S Y L U T J D
R V U G J X Y A W J H Y A Z D O G K P G
```

Solution on page 182

BE MINDFUL OF THE OTHER IN YOUR FRIENDSHIP

As with **everything** else in **life**, doing your **best** at **building** a **meaningful** relationship blesses you and your **friend**. When your friend is **suffering**, you listen with **empathy**, offer **encouragement**, and **validate** their **emotions** without judging them. In the **same** way, they **reciprocate** in your time of **need**. It's what friends do—**transmit** the **energy** of **kindness** to one another and take **comfort** in the **shelter** of their friendship. **True** friendship requires you to be fully **present** to your friend, mindful of self and **other**. The following walking **meditation** intensifies **mindfulness**.

1. **Calm** and **center** your mind as you set off on a walk to your friend's **house** or a **favorite** meeting **place** you two might share.

2. Walk with your thoughts **anchored** in the **here** and now.

3. **Place** your **hands** behind your **back**, right **palm** facing the **sky** and resting on top of your **left** palm with **thumbs** lightly **touching** (a variation of the **Buddhist** Dhyani Mudra, where the palms are in **front** of the body, the **right** hand symbolizing **enlightenment**, and the left, the **world** of **appearance**).

4. **Focus** on the **blessings** of your friendship with the other **person**.

5. Feel **gratitude** for those blessings.

6. **Hold** your friend in your **heart** as you stay mindful in the **moment**.

```
X I N F V M U H C G F I C T D W Z F V Z
O R T Z L N X V V V R E T L E H S A M E
A W R A U X G S B M U H T I M S N A R T
O M P X N R S V A L I D A T E N E R G Y
X T O E X L W U S S E N D N I K K P R E
B O E M R O E E C H O P L E R E H R V F
Y U G R E S Z B R O N U C M E D T E T I
A C R E I N O E G L F I D N M R R S F L
N H S H C I T N E D P L C E O Y N E E D
C I R T C N I C N F R O N T T S B N L B
H N X O E D A I R O U E I H I U L T I P
O G O C L L M R W R R R I G O F E R Q H
R E C I P R O C A T E N C I N F S U U A
E Q U H T S I G C E G G U L S E S E G N
D B I C I A E G J K P I U N F R I E N D
E A G N T M T Y H T A P M E K I N F G S
S C U R E V M I C T M E A N I N G F U L
U K A N T S I H D D U B Z L M G S K Y J
O E T I R O V A F E D U T I T A R G B V
H M L B A M L A C O M F O R T I V O P B
```

Solution on page 183

QUELL YOUR NEED
FOR NOISE

If you **always** have to **have** the **television** or the **radio** on, or if you always fall **asleep** to the television or to **music**, then you've **probably** got a noise **habit**. Noise can **temporarily** mask your **loneliness** or nervousness. It can **calm** an **anxious** mind or **distract** a **troubled** mind. **Constant** noise can **provide** a welcome **relief** from **oneself**, but if it is **compromising** your **ability** to think and **perform** as well as you could, if it is **keeping** you from **confronting** your stress and **yourself**, then it's **time** to make some **space** for **silence** in your life. Too much **noise** is **stressful** on the body and the **mind**. Give yourself a **break** and let yourself **experience** silence at **least** once **each** day for at least ten **minutes**.

```
O L H Y N K F B T E B K U E J F H V D E
C M X Y N D E L B U O R T O M A U V S Z
M K R Q H Q I N M G E C N E L I S P B M
W X K A K P L P H M A H K W E N T R R I
F E Y F U Y E A M R P T A K V X P O E H
O X P D N I R Q T K I Y S K L E F B A P
L O G L P M Y S S A S Q Y A A R X A K R
R R G N I S I M O R P M O C E Q P B D I
E A O P I D E G E S Q T H P C L K L J M
C D M H U T E L E V I S I O N A H Y S X
A I I I L J N J Y B A M U R K Y L T O A
P O Q V N E E O A V D H T Z T I R M N S
S A N G O U U H R E C N E I R E P X E L
U B T Z N R T N M F A C L A S N I N S E
I V N Q S H P E U T N I R S M O E V E E
Y K E E P I N G S Q B O F V U I C Y L P
T Q L I I F B N I A P U C S M S N H F G
H F G J V Q O P C M L C S S B E E D R A
K Z O V J C S S E N I L E N O L B T H H
I I Q N G V V T W X Z H P Q D Q C I E A
```

Solution on page 183

LOSING YOURSELF IN WORK

Throw yourself into your work, **mindful** of every **aspect** you **tackle**. For **instance**, you can be mindful of **typing**, focusing **completely** on the **document** in front of you **rather** than thinking about the **Internet** site you want to **check** before you **leave** for **lunch**. Losing **yourself** in your work is of course **easier** with some **tasks** than **others**. You will **probably** find it easier to **become** your work if you are doing **physical** work, **rather** than if you are working with **numbers** or **managing** a crowded **roomful** of people. You will **find** that if you can work in a **state** of mindfulness, you will **perform** the tasks at **exactly** the **level** they need to be performed. You will move **neither** too **slow** nor too **fast**; everything will be exactly as it **should** be. There is a **wonderful** freedom in **entering** fully into the **moment**. All of your **preconceptions** disappear. Your mind **opens** up and you have more **energy**. Your thoughts are not **draining** the life **force** from you as you **struggle** to **focus** on work when you'd rather be thinking about **dinner**. As your mind opens, your **concentration** expands, and you find your work gets done at a **higher** level, a level that you had been unable to **reach**.

```
K X B H S E R Z F M G E F K G D F L L J
H I V V E A D B L L D M O G G E B U O N
U S X M T L X H E V A L C Q W C H F G K
Y K N H C B G V S C S P U O O N P R E E
L L E E E T E G R L O K S O R A L E L A
G R T L P L K N U A U M U L H T Q D K Z
S F C C S O U I O R S F E O T S I N C P
N K R E A C H G Y A T A M C N N I O A X
K U S T E X X A G O V S S O X I M W T D
B L M A N T E N R E T N I N O P Q U M M
L R C B T E Y A E A A T C C L R E Y H R
H U D G E B M M N R P E R E H T I E N O
N V F N R R F U E E B F T N A M T S A F
X K O D I E S H C V T E O T E A S I E R
A M C T N F G N X O L B S R E N N I D E
R B O E G I O J C Y D Q L A C I S Y H P
B R E M H C M W A T C D O T H E R S C B
I C E V E C Q W O O D R A I N I N G N T
J A S R T N N W Y L B A B O R P H M U N
E F P T C P T D K R S A G N I P Y T L K
```

Solution on page 183

MAKING PEACE WITH YOURSELF USING MINDFULNESS

Self-acceptance is one of the **goals** in mindfulness meditation. When you **observe** the **thoughts** that **pass** through your mind, you **should** observe your reactions to them as well. What you may not **expect** is the **criticism** that you often level at **yourself**—for example, thinking "**wrong**" versus "**right**" thoughts about yourself or **others**, your **action** or lack of action in recalled **situations**. These **patterns** of thinking come from **conditioning** and past **experience**, and they are of no use in **growing** and **understanding**. Not judging yourself is difficult **enough**. But **when** the criticism and **high** expectations **diminish**, you need to **nourish** yourself. **Meditation** is a way of **addressing** that, but **insights** may come for **opening** your heart to the **fullness** of life you **seek**.

```
C S F X R H Y O U S V Z X O A H Y Z A N
R M I D J P W A B T O L R U B B P R O H
R G W T U Z R Q G S H O U L D H A I V R
E D N G U H E J P O E G Y F O Y T C E A
A G O I M A Q G B F F R I U R C T C T G
L H K A D S T J G D H O V R A B E Z N R
K F M P S N O I T A T I D E M P R I P M
I U W M C M A Z O Q P C N S B A N G O I
S L A O G S Q T C N A Q E S D O S R T E
B L D F R I S G S E S D I M I N I S H H
E N V Q A C N K C R S A Z T Y G O H E F
O E C N E I R E P X E D I O D U H S R Z
V S U M W T C E P X E D U V F W S T S I
K S T O Q I L S R L N R N X S O I H S Y
K X R W N R O O I O S E Y U P W R G F E
M G E J J C W R C E H S N E B R U U I C
N A Z U H Z A X L W V S N O D O O O B E
Z N V M P J O F Z P H I G H U N N H I J
Z T N D N Z F Y B E N N X C S G I T G N
N O D D Y S P G U G Q G G O I H H M B B
```

Solution on page 184

GET OUTSIDE AND MOVE

Walking is **great**. It's easy, **fun**, and can get you out in the **fresh** air or can **provide** an **opportunity** for **socializing** with **friends** while you all **shape** up **together**. Walk at a **brisk** pace for **thirty** to sixty minutes at least **three** times each **week**, and **preferably** **five** to **six** times per week. If you **feel** particularly **inspired** by great **views**, fresh air, and the **lovely** and **varied** smells of the **natural** world, **choosing** an **outdoor** exercise can inspire you to **keep** up the **habit**. **Whether** you walk, **jog**, run, **bicycle**, Rollerblade, cross-country ski, **hike**, or climb **mountains**, exercising outdoors is **good** for your **body** and **soul**.

```
Q V L Z I C Q D X I G N R Q F E Q A F Q
T G M I J C O H A Z E X O S R K H E A P
U T E K O O K V U N S I O B X U R G L X
Y G I R G K V S N V M Y D T A J L N U Y
B Q M B Y N V X E P A P T S E A R H E G
F P S C A R I B R F R M U E A P N W H I
U P H T C H B K O G Y O O M R U A T R Z
S E E D S A O R L T N M V U F E T H W X
Y C B E R S O C I A L I Z I N G U G S S
B L R I K P G N Z S W O S T D T R T O O
L F B R Q D U H L H K K O O A E A U V Z
E V I A K T Q O I L A G S R O E L I L W
O G J V R R V M E K E T N D R H E N N Q
Q G Q O S E R E H T E H W G N W C S B S
Y D P L L T F W H T V R E O S E Q P I N
F P T Y D O B E E T I E E Y P W I I A X
O C W U R R R A R D F E K P T H I R T Y
R W I V Q A O H D P T B I C Y C L E F O
C T R I J E H F X R W N H O T J E D T V
W P S P P O P R K X H R L F K R N B W N
```

Solution on page 184

BE A FRIEND TO
THE EARTH

Our **planet** earth is both awe-inspiring and **fragile**. Scottish-**American** naturalist John **Muir** declared, "The **clearest** way into the **Universe** is through a forest **wilderness**." With some **areas** of **forest** under threat, it's **perhaps** more **important** than ever to be a **friend** to the **earth**. **Nature** speaks **directly** to the **senses**—drawing you **outward** and **inward** at the same time and **fostering** a deep, **abiding** sense that the earth (which some see as a **living** entity) is due our **respect**, gratitude, **protection**, and **enduring** friendship. **Meditate** on ways you might **honor** and befriend the earth.

1. **Enter** meditation in Nature, **aligned** with the natural **world**, and be **fully** aware and **present** to it.

2. Feel **open**, serene, and **relaxed** as your senses **soak** up the **setting**.

3. Let your **awareness** take in the **sounds**, scents, and **sensations**, but don't get **caught** up. Instead **allow** your senses to **anchor** you into being fully **attentive** and present.

4. Sense the **interconnectedness** between you and your **setting**.

5. **Observe** how **sharp** your senses become as you sit in **mindful** awareness.

6. Allow Nature to **buoy** and nourish your **spirit** as you sink into the **rapture** of inner **quietude**.

7. **Feel** at one with all in your natural setting.

8. **Expand** your **consciousness** to include **Oneness** with all of Nature and then the Universe.

9. Feel **humbled**, inspired, and grateful to your friend, the earth.

```
D N R R S P A H R E P O E H M E B W M F
F R I E N D E W V T N E S E R P I U Z X
K N A A S R M R S E T G R U J L I N O H
A H Q N G P E A N X N E T N D R Q I N Y
O G V C Y S E E X I R P A E G N I V I L
S G D H B R S C R U A C R L F O R E S T
A N E O A S L E T R I N E L I G A R F A
I I X R U E T A N R E W H T R A E S C L
S T A U A S N V E S N O I T A S N E S U
O T L R O W B M S M U D R A W T U O E F
Y E E F P R A H S P R O T E C T I O N D
L S R O N O H R V E I C I Q O Q J D S N
T G N I R U D N E M V T U C R E T N E I
C Y D T E N A L P N K I K D S L V R S M
E I N T E R C O N N E C T E D N E S S D
R N V S P I R I T T M S M N A N O E Q L
I W G R A T E F U L L Y S G E L A C F R
D A P J A B I D I N G A S I Q T L P R O
G R X N V N E P O H U M B L E D T O X W
Q D T S O U N D S T H G U A C N I A W E
```

Solution on page 184

TRY OPTIMISM THERAPY

Optimism therapy is like an **attitude** adjustment but **focused** on **reframing** responses as an optimist. Optimism may have a **reputation** as a deluded **view** of the world through rose-colored glasses, but, actually, optimists are **happier** and **healthier** because they tend to **assume** they have **control** over their **lives**, while **pessimists** tend to feel that **life** controls them. Optimists are more **likely** to **engage** in **positive** behaviors such as **exercising** and **eating** well. Pessimists may adopt a **fatalistic** attitude that what they eat or how much they exercise doesn't **matter** anyway, so they **might** as well do what is easiest. But what if you are a pessimist? Can you **change**? Yes. You just **need** to engage in a **little** optimism **therapy**! Studies show that **smiling**, even when you aren't happy, can make you feel happy. **Pretending** to be an optimist can **actually** make you feel like one and can help your body **learn** to **respond** like an optimist too. If your pessimism is **temporary** or **recent**, you can probably **help** yourself through your own **personal** optimism therapy **sessions**. At the **beginning** of each day, before you get out of bed, say one of these **affirmations** out loud several times:

"No matter what **happens** today, I won't judge **myself**."

"**Today** I will **enjoy** myself in healthy **ways**."

"No matter what happens **around** me, this will be a **good** day."

Then, **choose** one **single** area or part of your day and **vow** to be an optimist in that **area** only. Maybe you'll choose **lunchtime**, or the staff **meeting**, or the time with your **kids** before dinner. During that **period**, every time you begin to think or say **something** pessimistically, **immediately** replace the words or **thought** with something optimistic.

```
E J D Z L I V E S D I K O V I S Y A W A
P G N I L I M S I N G L E G A R O U N D
W B O M O E K G N G G Y L L A U T C A O R
R K P Y R L C E N E N O G R N R A E L I I
O Y S S T Q I T L I P I O T W E I V H R
B G E E N Z T S R Y N P T D P T F I Y E
D N R L O O S E H O M N A E R T O T J P
E I E F C M I E I E Q Y I H E A C I L Z
K M I Q O H L T T Q X L J G T M U S I D
X A P J T P A D A P A E Y E E F S O Z P
D R P L M T T N F M E T R A N B E P N R
N F A S U E A I G I R A C C D L D E I Z
T E H P M P F N M E A I U H I O U R T F
H R E U C E L T T I L D F T N S T S H B
E R S D S S N O I S S E S F G A I O O M
R S P V L U N C H T I M E R A F T N U S
A Y O J N E P E S S I M I S T S T A G U
P W S O F S O M E T H I N G B M A L H L
Y K G I H E A T I N G E G A G N E R T D
J P L R E C E N T H G I M V G T I F H Z
```

Solution on page 185

CULTIVATE GRATITUDE

Think about something **someone** did for you, **something** touching and **unexpected**. It **might** be hard to think of it at **first**, but some act of **kindness** will **eventually** come to you. Maybe a **cashier** alerted you to a **discount** or **coupon** that you didn't know **about**, or **maybe** someone let you **take** their cab when you were in a **hurry**. Take a **moment** to think about how it felt to be on the **receiving** end of this **action**. **Cultivate** gratitude for this **random** act of kindness.

Then, pay it **forward**! Give up your **seat** on the **subway**, bake **cookies** for a new **neighbor**, pay for someone's **coffee** in the drive-through, or just give a **stranger** a heartfelt **compliment**. What you do is not **important**, as long as it is a **positive** act that is **intended** to **brighten** someone else's day. **Engage** in **small** acts of kindness as **often** as you can, and you'll **notice** a marked **increase** in your own well-being!

```
T D B R E C E I V I N G V A C G R B G G
P N N M G T H G I M T A D A U T X W H I
E V E N T U A L L Y D L I K Z K U J H A
F Y C M L K N V D C Q U L F X N O M Y S
U M C O I G I E I E T T V D B D T S G U
Y W U M U L M H X T Y B N E T H G I R B
E M M T R P P S V P L S T R A N G E R W
S X R A N D O M L S E U E C I I T O N U A
S F C O N M R N O T C C C H U R R Y K Y
M A Y B E Y T M L C U A T N U O C S I D
S E C O T N A E L L B E S E B L A E N D
V Q N O F N N O A E M J S H D K E A D Q
X E Q D O G T I M O V A G R I E T T N U
T K S L A K N N S V E I A L F E Z A E G
S N U G W S I T V R E W T F S D R O S H
R I E M Q Z V E C N R N O I T C A J S B
I H H M Q C R N S O A C Z M S Q E Z H L
F T J Y O L I D F G K Z D A B O U T R Q
W A L C E M D E K A T S S J S T P O S T
A C W P U A Y D F X D N D W D U I S M X
```

Solution on page 185

WHERE YOU SEE DARKNESS, SHINE A LIGHT

When **faced** with darkness, **become** a **beacon** of **light**. Be an **exemplar** of **humility**, civility, **patience**, compassion, **kindness**, sincerity, and—above all—**calmness**. **Cultivate** virtuous **qualities** so that they are always **part** of your **being**. Behaving with **benevolence** can turn a foe into a friend.

---

1. Sit with a **straight** spine. **Close** your eyes and **tune** in to your heart as you **breathe** naturally in a slow **pattern**.

2. **Visualize** a **beautiful** temple. See yourself crossing a **peaceful** lake that **washes** away all negativity as you **prepare** to enter the **temple**.

3. Let the temple light **embrace** you as the **inner** sound of **tinkling** bells **rings** out your presence.

4. **Touch** your **palms** together in the **Namaste Mudra** to greet the Divine **Presence** within.

5. Call **forth** an **individual** with **whom** you've had a negative **encounter**.

6. **Welcome** them into the temple's **sacred** space.

7. Feel the **energy** of the Divine in your **heart** chakra. Feel your whole body become energized as the **scent** of roses **permeates** the temple space, and **observe** the same light, **scent**, and energy surrounding the **person** you hold in your heart.

8. Observe how the darkness **dissipates** in the **numinous** presence of the Sacred.

9. **Fix** your thoughts on the **Divine** in all hearts.

10. **Rest** in the holy, **healing** light of **friendship**.

```
T E M P L E Z R D W P E R S O N H X M W
S G N I R K I N D N E S S B R E A T H E
Z D F A C E D T I C O L S U A Z H O X M
D T R A E H S B N T U E C L O G M E G Y
E M B R A C E E B E R L I O I N M J G M
R J Z D N N L A N V C N T L M P I R O E
C M K U Z O G U E C G S A I L E E M N C
A S Q M V L N T T F E L D A V N A U U B
S X E E Y U I I T R P E R M E A T E S N
U L N T Z K L F S I E N C O U N T E R E
D E P S A T K U E E N W C A L M N E S S
B Z Z A F P N L R N I D J O P L Y P T E
E I W M T H I N I D N T I U D T A A R H
I L S A B T T S V S N R I V I T A L A S
N A M N E G E V S H E A P L I F N M I A
G U E R A P E R P I R P I E A D O S G W
L S B E C O M E N P D M N H G U U R H V
F I X T O U C H P I U C L O S E Q A T I
F V V E N I V I D H E P E A C E F U L H
U T Q H I H X V N Z V L Z G L Z L X T J
```

Solution on page 185

BREATHING A CIRCLE OF LOVE

If you **project** a **straight** line into **space**, it eventually comes back as a **circle**. Love is like that too. The **adage** "What you **send** out **comes** back to you" is **true**. Send **love** to **others** and also **open** a channel to **draw** the flow of **Divine** Love into you, and you will **establish** a never-ending circle. The following **meditation** focuses on love as **characterized** by the **Buddhist** bodhisattva (someone who has **attained** enlightenment but remains **out-side** of **nirvana**—**freedom** from endless **cycles** of **birth** and death, **karma**, and suffering—until all others reach **enlightenment**).

1. Practice **alternate** nostril **breathing** until you feel **centered** and grounded.

2. Close your eyes and breathe **naturally**.

3. Rest in heart chakra awareness of a **warm** and loving **appreciation** of the Self.

4. Be **present** to how this **feels**, what this **means**. Do you need to **forgive** your-self or others to **completely** open your heart? Do you **need** to set a specific **intention**? If so, do that with an **affirmation**.

5. Draw your **focus** away from self-love into an **expansion** of consciousness that **embraces** love for all **beings**.

6. Breathe in and **visualize** a **golden** light filling your consciousness and **spread-ing** throughout your being.

7. Affirm: "I am a **channel** for Divine Love."

8. **Exhale** and visualize a **radiant** stream of **unconditional** love flowing outward in all **directions** from your heart.

9. Affirm: "My love is ever-expanding to **include** all beings."

10. **Imagine** unconditional love **flowing** in and out in an **unbroken** circle.

```
M Y N I R V A N A G O L D E N V A T D C
R Z S N D H Z T N A I D A R A I M N Z E
A X T C I E T B K S E M O C T S R E E X
W I R L V S R R L N C O Z N U U A S C H
O J A U I R O E I E K O E T R A K E A A
U H I D N E S A T B N K M D A L R R P L
T B G E E H T T V N O N E P L I P P S E
S Z H S D T D H O R E E A A L Z R D U A
I W T T A O E I B L N C N H Y E E R F O
D K S A K V T N R O E O S R C Z T F P S
E E I B O A U G I E I T J I I K I E F H
N I H L T S K S D T C T A R G R N Z L M
I N D I G E N L I G H T E N M E N T O Y
G T D S J A E D S F I T I A R X R D W O
A E U H P V N L O O C D T O B E E C I C
M N B X I O E C N A A I R V N E T E N Y
I T E G C E U D R E O L G A R S I L G C
K I R N F S K A R N C U F F W J F N A L
X O U J E E H P R O J E C T W A D A G E
F N K E K C S E C A R B M E L C R I C S
```

Solution on page 186

JUST SAY "OH WELL"

When you **feel** a rage, a **surge** of irritation, a **flood** of despair, or a **panic** coming on, one way to **circumvent** the surge is to **consciously** adopt a **passive** attitude. How? Two words: Oh well. These two **little** words are **extremely** powerful. You spilled your **coffee** on your **keyboard**? Oh well. **Something** is **broken**, wrecked, ruined? Oh well. Your **child** talks back? Oh **well**.

If your child **talks** back to you, that doesn't **mean** they shouldn't have to suffer the **consequences**, but it **also** doesn't mean you have to get all **worked** up about it. **Besides**, a **serene** parent **doling** out consequences is much **more** in **control** than a **flustered** parent.

If you make a **mistake**, learn from it. Something **happened**. You'll be more **careful** next time. But "oh well" means you **recognize** that attaching negative **emotions** to a mistake will **cloud** your thinking **rather** than **clear** it up. If you aren't **filled** with rage, you'll be **better** able to **respond** and **react** appropriately.

```
S E Z P S I C C J Z Q D V D A V T A M D
Q Q U D O U H I O O S L A C H U C L E Y
I P C M V I R N J N D E L L I F A R A J
O G Z G L T L N I B S Y D E W Y E W N L
L H O D T I B S H C E E C I F T R L T X
C Q Y Q N L P S A M J H Q E S U R G E T
F B J J C Z R R P O E D R U R E H Y A X
X L V P L A E P P R R D L G E P B L Z P
H G O Q O F S R E E F F O C C N K E P L
E T R O U K P G N I H T E M O S C M Y F
W U E L D Y O W E D B W Y J G N G E L R
A O H O I I N F D L R H C M N O C R S E
W H T R B C D C V L P A Z S I I M T U M
S B A T I W V J U E Y A O A Z T I X O O
W D R N M O I Z N W D B S B E O S E I Q
X C A O E R Z E L O V T E S Y M T E C I
U P E C K K R E L T T I L T I E A S S T
O U L U N E J I U U D Y Y I T V K T N B
F F C B S D N Z B N Z G A Q F E E L O L
G Y E S K G M P L T N E V M U C R I C H
```

Solution on page 186

Feeling stressed? Feeling **anxious**? Go on **vacation**. No, don't **leave** your desk and head to the **airport**. You **remember** your **imagination**, don't you? Your imagination is **still** in your **head**, even if it's **grown** a little **rusty** from disuse. **Stay** at your **desk**, close your eyes, **relax**, **breathe**, and use your imagination to **visualize** the **place** you would most like to be. Why not imagine **wandering** down a **secluded** beach at **sunset**, the balmy **tropical** winds **rippling** the **turquoise** sea? **Maybe** you would prefer **cuddling** in front of the **fire** with a **special** someone in a **cozy** cabin in the **woods**? Maybe images of the **Far East**, the rain **forest**, or **hiking** a glacier in **Alaska** evoke a **sense** of **peace** in you?

V P F Q O G K Q W K V X A Y K J R E U X
H F R H G I Y K K G L G A P F I A B K E
N U Z E H T A E R B R M M L M J E N O X
X W Q Q B T S F G Q S K U A E S N E S T
C T A N M M L I B P H A Z C T R T R E A
I M Z C D A E H I L A I C E P S U A L A
V V X L N P K M W P N O J K H Q E S Y L
V U U Q E N A O E N X G L N X D H R T B
W C B A W A N D E R I N G H W Y X V O Y
E O C I E H S P V M O S O Q I O O X U F
M E X R V T I Q A I U W F C C K R X C D
K Z S P A V R G D G S A O Z U E I G K G
W H L O E S I O U Q R U T O D M N N G R
D D L R L N T X P E F G A E D I S I G M
N O I T A C A V A I X J D L L S U L M A
O V P T K R Z S Y L C U M P I M N E G U
T O I S S B T K P P L A P T N Z S E M N
V O J Y A L Y Z O C Y I L T G E E F Z V
N J O W L F I R E B R A T M M Z T U A R
R B L I A I I S E M L D E S K W L T D K

Solution on page 186

LOVING-KINDNESS MEDITATION

According to **Buddhist** teachings, the **qualities** of love and **compassion** constitute the **foundation** for **ethics**, but it **starts** with loving-kindness toward the **Self**. Science **suggests** that compassion may have a **profound**, evolutionary **purpose** because we **humans** have **mirror** neurons that **react** to other people's **emotions** and **trigger** in us a **desire** to help. **Radiating** compassion without **discrimination** makes you **stronger** and more **resilient** and instills greater **happiness**. The following **meditation** guides you from loving-kindness toward yourself, to four other **people**, then to all **beings**.

1. Use a **breathing** technique to induce a **calm**, centered **state** of mind.

2. Offer a **prayer** such as "**I dedicate** the **virtues** of myself for the **benefit** of all."

3. Think of **four** people to **whom** you will send **love** and then **formulate** an **affirmation** to help you **arouse** loving-kindness in your **heart**: "I am **wanted** and loved. I **forgive** myself and others. I feel my heart **full** of love. I **hold** in my heart the **peace** of the **Divine**. My loves call forth love, peace, and **joy** in all hearts."

4. **Feel** the loving-kindness **toward** yourself.

5. **Visualize** each of the four people. Think of them **swaddled** in love, peace, and happiness as you radiate those feelings to **them**.

6. **Think** of the four **directions** the **wind** blows and then radiate love in all directions to beings of all **spheres** and **realms**.

```
G J K A A R E O D F K V N J P D H S R K
F H K N I H T S B G S E R E H P S E L F
K G A R O U S E N W N U E R I S E D N M
S E U T R I V S T O E I G T Z V I O O F
N H V K T A T Q R N I T H G A R I H I L
A L A R E R J A U E O T A T E T W F T Q
M E A P A G L E N A Y I O C A S S P A Z
U E Q T P N V J N I L A T M I E T E D H
H F S G N I E B O V M I R A E D R S N R
D F L E G T N T I Y O I T P T L E B U E
X S O R T A S E S N F R R I O I P D O C
B R O R R I M S S F X F E C E T D O F A
J F D H H D W S A S O B S A S S A E E E
C L O D H A T O P R N Q I L C I L J M P
S L D Y D R U U M R E A L M S T D O F T
D U P D O I R U O Y E Z I L A U S I V H
B F L N H P L J C T I F E N E B F B Z E
M E G F O A P R O F O U N D R A W O T M
D E T S T R I G G E R E T H I C S D U P
R Z E E N I V I D E T N A W I N D J C R
```

Solution on page 187

SLEEP MEDITATION

You may **find** yourself lying **awake** at **night**, not **knowing** what to do in order to get to **sleep**. The following brief **meditation** will **help**. It's **easier** to fall asleep when your body is **relaxed**. **Naturally**, this is difficult to **achieve** when you are worried and tense. But **simple** muscle-toning **exercises** can help. **Pranayama** exercises (**conscious** breathing) should **accompany** a sleep med-itation because the **assistance** they **render** is invaluable. Good **oxygenation** will **induce** a relaxed **state** and encourage **yawning**—always a **good** sign.

Lie on your **back**, hands on **stomach**, legs **extended**, eyes half closed. Avoid **curling** your body in a ball or **lying** on your side. **Gradually** focus on your body, from the **feet** up. **Focus** your **attention** only on your **bodywork**. Starting with the feet, **turn** them in and curl your toes **downward**, as tight-ly as **possible**. As you do this, **inhale**. Release **slowly** while **exhaling**. Move to your **calves**, turn them **inward** and tighten the **muscles** while inhaling. **Release** slowly while exhaling. Now focus on your **thighs**, tightening the muscles while inhaling. Release slowly while exhaling. Move your attention to the **torso**. As you inhale, allow your stomach to **expand** fully. Slowly exhale. **Tensing**, release your hands while inhaling and exhaling. Do the same with your arms and hands, while **raising** your **shoulders** upward toward your ears. Inhale; exhale while tensing and releasing. Tense your **head** by raising your **chin** upward as far as possible while inhaling. Slowly release it downward while exhaling. Avoid **twisting** your neck to the **right** or **left**. Perform three conscious breaths while **wriggling** your **fingers** and **toes**.

```
D D T D M H B H C A M O T S S I M P L E
G G O O S Q J E C U D N I J E X P A N D
I N G O R F I N G E R S T Z V N S H J N
G I Q T G S U E S A E L E R L Z F E T I
M N R H N F O C U S Z M I L A K S L O F
L W E I I E X T E N D E D N C A H P O T
H A I G L E Y L L A U D A R G S O S A U
F Y S H G T G J M V M W X A I S U S M R
T F A S G N E N K E A Z C X S O L M A N
U W E R I H N C D K L C N I I O D S Y G
L L I W R S A I E O O O B C W R E H A E
P Y O S W B T Y S M I L S L A D R E N R
G N I G T A I A P T E N Y W Z E S A A K
K N Q N T I O A N A O T N E E P T D R A
I U I I G P N E N C H I N D V U E A P Y
I N O S N Y T G I S E S I C R E X E T Y
L N H I N T J O D O W N W A R D I D L S
E X G A A E J G Q G N I L A H X E H O S
F H E R L E T D E X A L E R I G H T C B
T R E N D E R B O D Y W O R K L W I D A
```

Solution on page 187

BE OPEN TO CHANGE

Becoming more **open** to **change** is an **attitude** shift. Start **spotting** changes and then finding one **good** thing about every change you **experience**. Someone **parked** in your spot? You can get an **extra** few minutes of **exercise** by **walking** from a spot **further** away. It's good for your **body**! Your **favorite** television **show** is pre-empted? Another **opportunity**! Spend the **evening** reading a **book** or taking a walk or **practicing** a new stress **management** technique. **Major** changes are even **easier**. Any change, no **matter** how disturbing to you, can have its **positive** side, even if you can't **find** it right **away**. But finding the positive **side** isn't even the most **important** thing. The most important thing is a **willingness** to **accept** that, yes, **things** change and, **yes**, you can go with the **flow**.

```
F Z Z N D M W S T I B K J S V J C I I C
F F D Q M K S W K O J D E D M A T K D X
V O L W K A Z R G L K S H O W Q C L Q Q
K G W Y E I M I T N A T R O P M I E Z Q
C F H Y D W N W N V I H H G N U X W A E
V X M I H Y J F E E N M I E V E N I N G
V Z U N W L A O M E O E O K R H T C S O
G H U Q O G Y F E C G S V C S S F B D W
N N W A L K I N G N S X I R E H T R U F
I E I P F F M Y A E D S B Y B B O O K X
T G P C F L D H N I E T I R O V A F X U
T A T O I R C G A R E I S A E B I M R H
O M E Q N T N M M E Y A J X P Y S O E Q
P X D A D I C R Z P O O T I O G A U T U
S E U W L Q X A Z X L R J M U A O W T C
G B T L W L J G R E A R D E K R A P A P
Y T I N U T R O P P O S I T I V E R M Z
D W T H I N G S B J P I V M X C H A T P
O X T C T W G X A V D D D I C J E B U C
B X A B W A R M B H Q E W A S G T U L C
```

Solution on page 187

Clutter creates **stress**. Just **looking** at clutter **suggests** clutter to the mind. While decluttering your **entire** garage, **basement**, or **bedroom** closet may be a **monumental** task to **accomplish** all at **once**, any big decluttering job can be accomplished in **small** steps. **Every** day, spend **five** or **ten** minutes—no **more**, unless you **schedule** ahead to **spend** a larger **block** of **time**—decluttering **something**. Maybe it will be that dump-it **table** by the **front** door, or the **pile** of **laundry** on top of the **dryer**, or one **corner** of your **desk**. Whatever it is, **clear** something out once each **day** and **feel** your **mind** let out a **sigh** of **relief**.

```
M W L P T P O S M V A A S A G S W R U R
Y A G A G T T L F P R K K W O I I H K G
A J X A N W A Q A I S A W L D J D Y K O
P M E K Z U I E W T U I E V E R Y A U H
R A R L N T E L S C N I G E I E Y A Q X
L Q H D M K Z E R O M E N H M L X E D C
F F R I N I G K A C C O M P L I S H R Q
I Y C N I G N B P V F Q U U G E T N E T
K R T J U X I D B Q C R X L N F C L Q V
A L B S I Z K L T K M O O M I O B N S E
K S Y S Y K O X U H R D R N H A M C O G
V U E M N C O V R A E L C N T Q N O Y D
N R Q U K T L G A S R E T N E M E S A B
F A R I A P B D K V I E H Z M R L R O E
Z F O U P X V E S W T F T S O Q U S D D
W S R E J P F M J S N J Y T S Q D U B R
M M K T H I A C D N E P S Y U H E C D O
T O S A D L L A K K V R G F M L H T Q O
X F D B L E T H V P I M T T D U C W J M
W U W E A F Q B Z D F T X S Q I S I B H
```

Solution on page 188

TAKE A RISK

As **scary** as it can be to try a new **activity** or step **outside** of your **comfort** zone, it's **worth** the effort. Trying new **things** and **taking** small **risks** is **vital** to your well-being. Have you been **considering** taking a **dancing** lesson? Do you **stare** longingly at the **happy**, healthy **people** stretching in the **yoga** studio as you **walk** by? Are you both **excited** and **terrified** by the **prospect** of signing up for a speed-dating event? **Instead** of convincing yourself that **branching** out isn't worth the **effort** and **courage** required, **challenge** yourself to **follow** through on one of your **unfulfilled** desires.

Commit to doing at least one new, **intimidating** thing **every** day. Taking a risk can be as **small** as **striking** up a **conversation** with someone you don't **know** or as **large** as accepting a job **offer** in a **different** country. The **point** of this exercise isn't to **radically** alter your **life**, but to **develop** a **habit** of trying new things and **opening** yourself up to all the **possibilities** that life has to offer. The **next** time you find yourself **talking** your more **adventurous** side out of accepting an **invitation** to **karaoke** night or coming up with **excuses** to get out of a **volunteering** opportunity with a **friend**, stop and ask yourself why you are **avoiding** something that you might **enjoy**. If the **answer** is **simply** that you are scared to take a risk, **push** yourself to **overcome** your fear and dive **headfirst** into the **uncertainty**!

```
T H I N G S H P F Q K A N K W O R T H J
A Y P P A H S U O R U T N E V D A R Y P
K C O N V E R S A T I O N O X Y Z T O E
I D S M A L L H T S W M L G W T D L J R
N A S V W L N N I U R U N E C I E E N A
G N I T A D I M I T N I X E F V U M E T
X C B I Q O P F E T R C P F E I N O G S
R I I M P L Z R E E I S E D Y T F C N R
T N L M Y Y R E D T O R M R F C U R I I
R G I O Q I R I E R E I B E T A L E N F
O Q T C F I S D P N N W R W E A F V E D
F Z I I N N D V T S O R A S K I I O P A
F B E G O N W G T L F B N N O T L N O E
E D S C E G N E L L A H C A A E L O T H
X C E I Y I A O T I B A H T R G E F R Y
C D R R K D F Y L L A C I D A R D F O G
U F E I J E D I S T U O N E K A T E F S
S V R Y A V O I D I N G G W A L K R M K
E T A L K I N G P E O P L E G A R U O C
S K S I R L A T I V U B A G O Y R A C S
```

Solution on page 188

LOVE BY ANY OTHER NAME

The **ancient** Greeks had a **thing** or two to say about **love**, and one **word** wouldn't do. In fact, they had **six** words for love: *eros*, *philia*, *ludus*, *pragma*, *philautia*, and *agape*. Eros **signified** the **passionate** kind of love that takes **possession** of your **senses**, while **philia** symbolized the **deep** and **loyal** love between **comrades** who **would** lay down their lives for each **other**. Ludus was the **kind** of love **exhibited** by **frisky** young lovers, as opposed to **pragma**, the **enduring** bonds of love that **empower** couples to have a long **married** life. Philautia, or self-love, was **viewed** two ways by the **Greeks**: **narcissism** (not desirable) and self-love that increased your **capacity** for loving others. Agape, the **highest** form, was a **selfless** love for all **people**. This **meditation** reminds you to remove **barriers** to the flow of love— whatever name you call it.

1. Sit in your **favorite** asana. **Calm** your mind.

2. **Reflect** on how love **perfects** human **relationships**.

3. **Consider** how love **holds** you.

4. **Think** about how you love others.

5. **Dissolve** walls, boundaries, and **limitations** you may have **erected** to feel safe.

6. Let love **flow** easily without barriers.

7. **Mentally** affirm: "I am **meant** to love and be loved, to become **whole** and **holy** as love flows to and **through** me."

```
B F L O W Z V B P V I O T H E R G M D D
M A R R I E D H D E E P H Y P J R R E C
K N R I K K I G N R L H I L A O E W U O
C Q S R S L U D U S O H N L G L E T X M
G M L M I K X P N L H W G A A I K J E R
N E O A Y E Y O D I W T K T V P S D Z A
I D V J N J R S R V K N I N L B I D O D
R S E N S E S S D S I O K E Z T X P T E
U O O B A T S E K H N Q T M A M M N S S
D R W E L R I S T S P O S T C E F R E P
N E G O X F C S H E X H I B I T E D L T
E R Y K I N E I C W C O I T B I N C F G
V A L N C H P O S O N A E L A U W A L V
L P G Y G S R N Q S N T P P A T X L E F
O I R I L E T A N O I S S A P U I M S M
S D H A W O U L D R G S I J C E T M S F
S U M O G T H R O U G H M D E I O I I K
I D P U H M N V P L A N C I E N T P A L
D M L A I K A U R D D E T C E R E Y L N
E T C E L F E R L V F V H L W K O W P E
```

Solution on page 188

ANSWERS

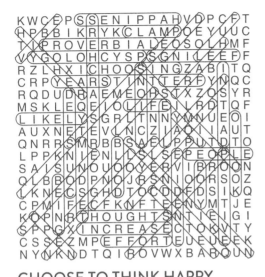

CHOOSE TO THINK HAPPY THOUGHTS

AWAKENING: THE ALTERNATING BREATH

THREE TIMES A DAY, VISUALIZE ACHIEVING A PERSONAL GOAL

SMILE MORE OFTEN

FEEL LIFE FORCE

PRAISE YOURSELF

165

HEALING ON ALL LEVELS

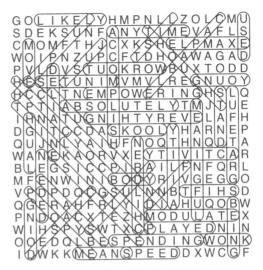

CONSIDER WHAT YOUR BODY CAN DO

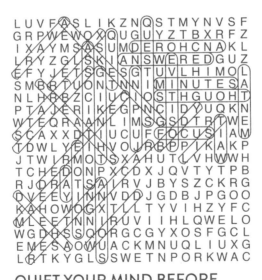

QUIET YOUR MIND BEFORE STARTING YOUR DAY

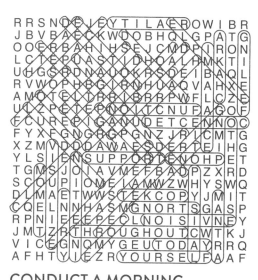

CONDUCT A MORNING
CHAKRA CHECK-IN AND
INTENTION-SETTING RITUAL

PHOTOGRAPHY AS
MANIFESTATION

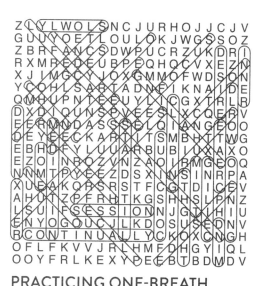

PRACTICING ONE-BREATH
MEDITATION

RETREAT WITHIN TO CLEAR YOUR MIND

NOURISH YOUR INNER BEING

EMBRACE PLEASANT SENSATIONS

OUTDOOR MEDITATION

SAVOR THE LITTLE MOMENTS

LISTEN CAREFULLY

**RELEASE THE PAST AND
APPRECIATE THE PRESENT**

**DESIGNATE ONE CORNER OF
YOUR HOME AS SACRED SPACE**

COMMITTING TO ANOTHER

HAVE A CONVERSATION WITH YOUR PAST SELF

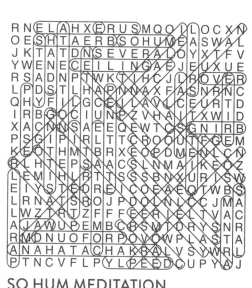

SO HUM MEDITATION

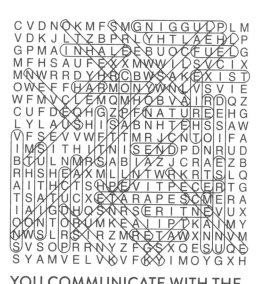

YOU COMMUNICATE WITH THE UNIVERSE

THE GIFT OF IMAGINATION

A NEW HABIT BEGINS WITH INTENTION AND RESOLVE

FIVE PURIFICATION BREATHS

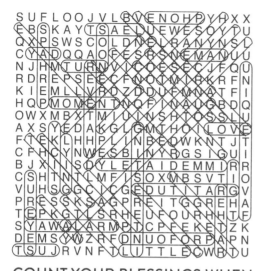

COUNT YOUR BLESSINGS WHEN YOU WAKE UP

MAKE A TEN-POINT LIST OF WHAT'S REALLY IMPORTANT TO YOU

CREATE A NEW TRADITION WITH YOUR FAMILY

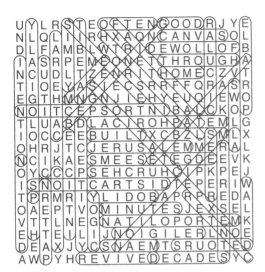

WALKING THE LABYRINTH

CHAKRA HEALING CAN ILLUMINATE YOUR LIFE PATH

MEDITATE WITH CRYSTALS FOR HEALING

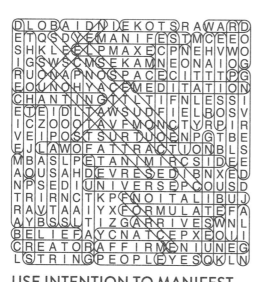

USE INTENTION TO MANIFEST SOMETHING DESIRED

TAKING IN THE COLORS OF THE NATURAL WORLD

A VISUAL MEDITATION

USE INTENTION TO DISCOVER YOUR LIFE'S PURPOSE

DAYDREAM FOR TWENTY MINUTES EVERY MORNING

HOW MANTRAS WORK

DON'T LET THIS MOMENT PASS YOU BY

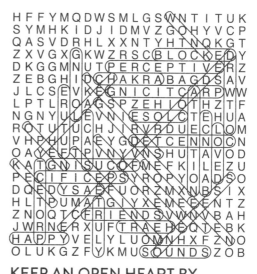

KEEP AN OPEN HEART BY WISHING OTHERS WELL

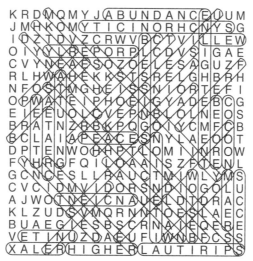

THE POWER OF INFINITE POSSIBILITY

USE A GRATITUDE REMINDER

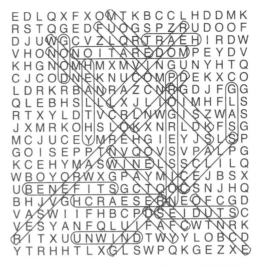

HAVE A GLASS OF WINE AT THE END OF A DIFFICULT DAY

VOLUNTEER AT AN ANIMAL SHELTER

THE SERENE MIND ENGENDERS JOY

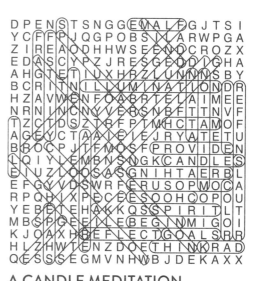

A CANDLE MEDITATION

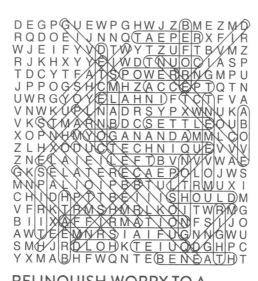

RELINQUISH WORRY TO A HIGHER POWER

COUNT YOUR LOOSE CHANGE AND DONATE IT

A MINDFUL EXERCISE

KEEP YOUR PROMISES TO OTHERS

EVERYDAY MOVING MEDITATIONS

ENJOYING THE PROCESS

MINDFULNESS VERSUS CONCENTRATION

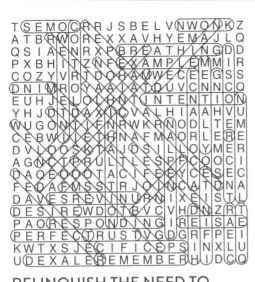

RELINQUISH THE NEED TO CONTROL

A COMMUTER'S MEDITATION

GIVE YOURSELF A BEDTIME

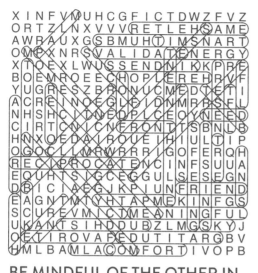

BE MINDFUL OF THE OTHER IN YOUR FRIENDSHIP

QUELL YOUR NEED FOR NOISE

LOSING YOURSELF IN WORK

MAKING PEACE WITH YOUR-
SELF USING MINDFULNESS

GET OUTSIDE AND MOVE

BE A FRIEND TO THE EARTH

TRY OPTIMISM THERAPY

CULTIVATE GRATITUDE

**WHERE YOU SEE DARKNESS,
SHINE A LIGHT**

185

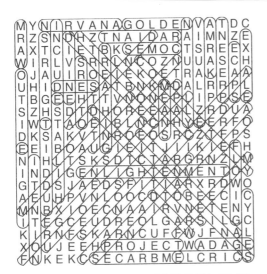

BREATHING A CIRCLE OF LOVE

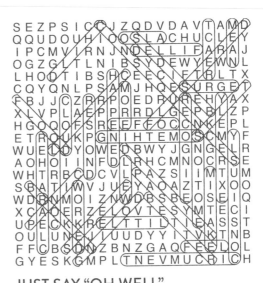

JUST SAY "OH WELL"

HARNESS IMAGERY POWER

**LOVING-KINDNESS
MEDITATION**

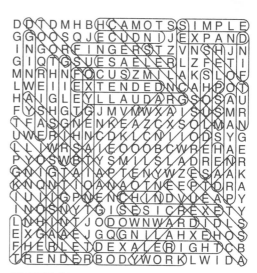

SLEEP MEDITATION

BE OPEN TO CHANGE

DECLUTTER YOUR LIFE

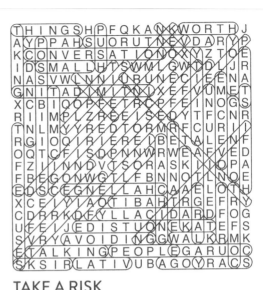

TAKE A RISK

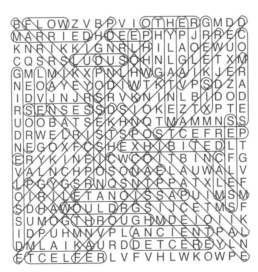

LOVE BY ANY OTHER NAME

Take your mindfulness to the next level
with these serene puzzles!

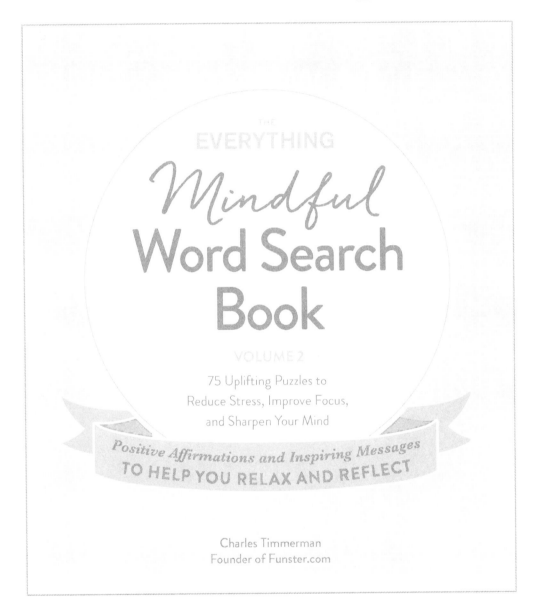

THE
EVERYTHING

Mindful
Word Search
Book

VOLUME 2

75 Uplifting Puzzles to
Reduce Stress, Improve Focus,
and Sharpen Your Mind

Positive Affirmations and Inspiring Messages
TO HELP YOU RELAX AND REFLECT

Charles Timmerman
Founder of Funster.com

Pick Up Your Copy Today!

adamsmedia
An Imprint of Simon & Schuster
A ViacomCBS COMPANY